Online Reputation Management: Secrets from a Pro Ethical Hacker

Fernando Uilherme Barbosa de Azevedo

Table Of Contents

Table Of Contents 2

About the Author 3

Introduction 4

Chapter 1: Online Reputation Management – What it is and What It Isn't 6

Chapter 2: A Closer Look at Offline and Online Reputation Management 9

Chapter 3: The Need for ORM – Why Online Reputation is Important 14

Chapter 4: Online Reputation Management (ORM) vs. Search Engine Optimization (SEO) 19

Chapter 5: ORM General Rules and Tools that can Help You Monitor Your Online Image 21

Chapter 6: Things You Need to Understand About Online Reputation Managers 26

Chapter 7: Simple ORM for the Unsophisticated Net User 31

Chapter 9: Best Examples of Successful ORM 42

Chapter 10: Your Ultimate Guide in Creating Good Online Reputation 46

Chapter 11: Sample Cases of Failed ORM 55

Chapter 12: Reputation Management Mistakes to Avoid 65

Chapter 13: FAQs Regarding Ways to Eliminate Negative Search Results 73

Chapter 14: The dark side of Online Reputation Management 78

Chapter 15: Cyber Criminals and Your Online Reputation 87

Final Words 92

About the Author

Fernando Uilherme Barbosa de Azevedo is an electronic, electrical and industrial engineer graduated from Pontifícia Universidade Católica of Rio de Janeiro. He is MBA graduate from Fundação Getúlio Vargas. He has been a programming instructor at Pontifícia Universidade Católica of Rio de Janeiro for 7 years.

He published his first book "Macros for Excel hands on" by publisher Campus/Elsevier at age 27. The book is still sold in Brazil and Portugal.

His first startup business won a prize from the Brazilian Federal Institutional FINEP.

Coming to the United States in 2014, Fernando studied Web Development and Internet Technologies at University of California Santa Cruz - Silicon Valley Extension and also completed the "Innovation and Entrepreneurship Certification" from Stanford University.

Fernando has been featured many times in news media and TV. He was interviewed as a specialist on his field by Forbes, The Entrepreneur, el Nuevo Herald and many other major Brazilian media companies.

Today, Fernando runs 2 internet marketing companies in the United States and has clients in many countries. The companies offer services such as internet marketing, Search Engine Optimization (SEO), Online Reputation Management (ORM), pen testing, systems audit, e-commerce, apps and other internet related activities.

He is also a web development instructor for IronHack and weekly speaker at Radio Gazeta.

Fernando considers himself an ethical hacker and thinks that the internet should be a safer place. By advocating against all the unethical activities online that are still present today, he hopes that our leaders and law makers can become aware of these threats and help create laws for a safer world.

This book is a series of 5 books related to Internet Technologies and how the internet works. If you like this book, please check out other books from the same author.

Introduction

We want to thank you and congratulate you for downloading *Online Reputation Management: Secrets from a Pro Ethical Hacker*.

We do business with those we trust. To gain trust, you need to be explicit about our passion that creates a better world and help people. Your genuine passion that you offer to the world makes a product or service great! And people will follow, like you, defend you and do business with you.

When people are evaluating you, they look for 6 persuasions rules: Reciprocity, Commitment and consistency, Authority, Social Proof, Scarcity and Liking to guide them.

If you gather 5 to 10 friends to look and point at a dot in the sky, you will soon been surrounded by people looking at the sky too.

Tourism in Venice has been high just because we keep seeing news it's going down under water.

We are willing to obey a men in a uniform even though his uniform might be just a costume for a party.

Websites offer free ebook and street sellers offer roses so you can feel like they helped you and know they deserve something back.

If you agree with those those paragraphs above, you will probably like the rest of this book.

This book is about creating, maintaining, managing reputation day to day and also reputation crisis. We are internet marketing professionals with over 10 years of experience and we have managed online reputations of dozens of politicians, celebrities and business men. We wrote this book to help you gather tools and techniques to help you navigate the reputation of your company and clients on the internet. We will be uncovering secrets that most people never knew it existed.

It intends to give you everything you need to know regarding online reputation management. Learn its importance, benefits, advantages, and other significant things. This book will take you behind the scenes and will let you take a glimpse at the fascinating world of online reputation management. Discover how to turn a negative image or reputation.

This book will help you:

- Understand what online reputation management is and some of its common misconceptions.

- Explain the similarities and slight differences between offline and online reputation management.

- See the benefits and importance of online reputation management.

- Understand ORM and SEO differences and similarities.

- Absorb the lessons from real cases of failed ORM.

- Learn the techniques in creating good online reputation.

- Determine the reputation management mistakes that you need to avoid.

- Eliminate the negative search results.

- Get to know the 'dark world' of Online reputation and some tools.

- Protect your online reputation against cyber criminals.

This book will guide on the latest techniques you never knew it existed. Campaign managers, celebrity managers, and marketing professionals will surely benefit from the guidance, tips, and vast information contained in every chapter of this book. If you want to build or maintain a good online reputation, you'll need this book to guide you.

Thanks again for downloading this book, I hope you enjoy it!

Fernando Uilherme Barbosa de Azevedo

Chapter 1: Online Reputation Management – What it is and What It Isn't

Possessing a good reputation is important for everyone, especially if you are a businessperson, blogger, celebrity, politician, or anyone whom the masses look up to. Type your name on Google's search bar or any other search engine and discover how you appear to the online community, which includes social networking sites, news sites, different forums, blog sites, search engines, and others. Is it good, bad, or just so-so? Do you think you are being represented fairly? Would you like to improve your image and reputation? Would you like to know how?

There are companies that offer services on reputation management and help you acquire a good online presence. You can also try to do it yourself, but you need to understand and learn the process thoroughly. An amateur may find it challenging to do at first, but it gets less complicated with a bit of practice and as you get to know more about it. You need to have patience and discipline when you try to learn new things and aim to be proficient on the said subject.

What it is in General

The primary task or goal of online reputation management or ORM is to control and influence the group's or person's reputation. ORM can help you take control of the online conversation. The techniques and strategies that ORM uses can help ensure that people who search for you in the internet will find the correct stuff.

A good online reputation management can give you the ability to put your best foot forward, cancel out misleading trend, and establish balance. ORM can help business owners create a good reputation and positive image for their brand within the online community.

If you own and manage a brand, you need to be mindful. It is imperative to know exactly what's going on with your brand. Gather information about its status and people's thoughts about it. Focus on the things they talk about when they mention your brand, product, or things you offer.

Many online communities and electronic markets like Alibaba, e-Bay, and Amazon have built in ORM systems. They also have efficient control nodes that can help lessen the threats and shield the system against potential abuses and misuses in decentralized overlay networks perpetrated by malicious nodes.

In this digital age, consumers rely on online sources to provide them with information they need regarding certain brand, company, service, or product. They prefer a company with good reputation. A well-designed online presence brings wonderful things to the business, and a grave negative review may cause irreparable damage.

Common Misconceptions

Online reputation management also has its share of common misconceptions. Establishing a good online reputation is challenging and maintaining a positive image is even more taxing.

1. People will only be interested to discuss your brand or things you offer if you already obtained a large scale online presence.

This is not true because consumers can always find ways to express themselves or communicate with one another online. Even a lesser local business owner knows that a simple comment of their client on Facebook regarding his/her experience with the company can spread to hundreds of possible clients.

2. You can ignore unfavorable reviews or comments about you.

Whether you are a business owner, blogger, celebrity, or anyone who should keep a good reputation within the online community, understand that ignoring the negative things that people say about you won't make them disappear. You may choose to close your eyes to avoid reading them and deny their existence, but they will remain visible to the entire online community. You can only lessen the damage if you have effective and viable response to stop people from discussing the issue further. A proper response is the only way to show your willingness to appease the frustration of your customer and display your sincerity in wanting to obtain your client's satisfaction. When potential clients read your response, you may even gain more customers.

3. It is easy to turn a negative reputation into a positive one within the online community.

A negative reputation is something that is quite challenging to reverse, regardless if it's online or offline. You need to take good care of your image if you want to succeed in your endeavor. It is important to begin managing your online presence from day one and not wait for a great disaster to occur before you decide to build a good image for yourself and your business. The primary mission of online reputation management is to make sure that your reputation never falls below positive line. Dealing with all the negative comments or reactions in a timely manner and identifying the problems before they escalate into something big can help quash their unfavorable effects to your image.

4. To stay on top, your business must only get 5/5 reviews all the time.

Many business owners believe that their online reputation must be at its peak all the time and that means getting a 5 out of 5 reviews from each client. Having a perfect five overall rating is rather suspicious. It appears unrealistic in the eyes of your customers and potential clients. The online communities expect that some people will not be pleased with your brand. Make sure that your brand has balanced reviews and favorable rating.

5. Reputation and search engine optimization don't have any relation.

Search engine optimization or SEO plays an important role in ORM. SEO can help mold the information into something that can help boost the image of a brand when the net surfers try to search about it. A local company that ignores the importance of SEO may face the risk of having unfavorable response when the first things that a potential client sees when he/she tries to Google about that company are the negative reviews or comments. First impression usually lasts, and you don't want your potential clients to have a bad image of your company in their minds.

6. Online reputation management takes care of bad reviews by generating more good reviews.

While fabricating loads of good reviews to hide or offset the bad reviews may cover some tracks, there are some causes that needed to patched. Plus, having honest reviews are still better than generating fake ones. The online communities are intelligent and may detect that something is off. The best way to counter a negative review is to understand the reason or cause for such review and explaining what you can do to meet the satisfaction of your client. You can ask for a second chance, review your processes and offer a deal to remove the bad review.

7. Your offline presence won't get affected by your online presence.

When a client is mesmerize and want to show what a good deal he found, he can often choose to do so on the internet. And when the client is angry and seek revenge, he will also find the internet the most powerful tool to harm your brand. Interactions and constant communications are vital to business growth, specially when you can encourage a good review or fix a mistake not to get a bad one. People who discuss almost anything in social media are not different from those who meet up and talk things over lunch or dinner, but, when online, the damage can stay there and reach and influence millions.

8. The company's employees won't contribute to the success or possible downfall of a company or business.

On the contrary, whatever your employees say or do may affect your company. You can rely on your employees (as well as their friends and family) to fortify the online reputation of your company. Likewise, anything bad they do online may also affect your company's image when people are aware that they work for you. Remind your employees to be mindful of the things they post on social media, especially if it's something that involves the company.

Don't wait for your reputation to suffer damages before you act, you must design a plan now to protect the image that you want to keep.

Chapter 2: A Closer Look at Offline and Online Reputation Management

A PR (offline) firm can't be considered the same as ORM firm and vice versa, although their main function is somewhat similar (that is to create positive image or reputation). ORM firms are content-oriented and technical while PR firms are personal or relationship-based. You can say that ORM firms can provide support to PR firms when needed.

People tend to mix up public relations or PR and online reputation management. It is not surprising since both share similarities. Remember that ORM usually works on stealth mode and PR prefers to do things in the open. ORM and PR can support each other.

Understanding Public Relations

The Public Relations Society of America defined public relations as a process in strategic communications that aims to establish beneficial relationships between the masses and the organizations. Simply put, the goal of public rations is to make the public image of a brand, organization, or person look good in the eyes of the masses.

As much as possible, its reactive and proactive parts must be equal or balanced. A thorough analysis of the entity's relationship with the masses must first be conducted before presenting or creating a good PR. Damage control or crises prevention is part of a good PR. It is to ensure that a certain problem won't create further damage on the image of a person or brand.

The principal components of public relation campaigns are:

- Complete assessment of how you appear in the public's eye, potential or target clients, among peers, and others. It creates an honest presentation of your strong and weak points (the research phase of online reputation management has a similar purpose when it comes to your digital presence).

- Policies that must be observed all the time when making public communication to limit off-brand or unsanctioned testimonial that company associates, or employees make (a training is usually required).

- Plans that clearly state the goals and objectives for the campaign, encompassing everything from the actual promotion or presentation to spending.

- Corporate or personal branding.

- PR may include:

> a. Reaching out to industry luminaries, patrons of the company or business, bloggers, and other personalities or groups that are known to be efficient influencers or information disseminators.
>
> b. Interviews conducted by media.
>
> c. Giveaways and contests that effectively instigate participation, promotions or sponsorships, and customer brand loyalty.
>
> d. Setting up events and public functions.
>
> e. Campaigns in the social media (also one of ORM's core functions).
>
> f. Disclosures and statements that must be known to the public, typically through the media.
>
> g. Press releases stressing any or all of the given points.

A number of PR's processes, tactics, and components are labor-intensive.

More on Online Reputation Management

You already know about what ORM is and its common misconceptions. If PR wants to be on the spotlight, ORM is more on the quiet side. Although ORM usually operates on stealth mode, it can generate merciless moves.

PR campaigns and ORM campaigns are quite similar, but the latter is more technical than the former. ORM campaigns commonly include all or some of the following:

- PR campaigns that lean toward the technical aspect.

- Complete research on the pre-campaign online reputation condition of the brand, company, or person as well as risk analysis.

- Content creation and supervision for:

    a. blog posts

    b. guest posts

    c. multimedia

    d. social content

    e. white papers

    f. others

- Removal of content.

- Development of controllable third party sites, social media, blogs, websites, and others (also known as web properties).

- Continuing campaign or endorsement of content and web properties in social media and search engines.

- Re-targeting of content to keep up with the changes in the behavior of search engine.

- Marketing and SEO (Search Engine Optmization).

- Efficient publication and broadcasting of completed content as scheduled.

Here are the typical ORM activities:

1. Drawing the attention of social media followers and creating buzz.

Once it has successfully attracted the attention of followers of social media and made some noise, producing brand advocates that can generate traffic or followers to web properties will be easy. It will be a cinch to generate social mention that can help enhance your reputation and reinforce SERP (search engine result page) standings.

2. Enhancing the SEO value of web properties, aiming to get higher SERP (earch engine results page) mentions, and presenting impeccable positive content.

3. Generating additional web properties that can also be extra sources of content that can help enhance the brand's image or reputation.

4. Handling online review sites (like Yelp), emphasizing the favorable scores and positive comments while being careful not to affect the objectivity.

Between traditional advertising and peer recommendation, at least 75% net users put their faith on the latter rather than the former as revealed in a Pew Statistics report not long ago.

5. Enhancing, supervising, and tracking the performance of all paid for, earned, and owned content channels.

6. Reaching out to and establishing content-producing partnerships with influencers in a field.

7. Directly making responses to some online messaging.

8. Submitting requests to take down (within relevant customs and laws) online publishers post information that are defamatory or inaccurate.

9. Taking legal action when necessary.

You may use all the said actions or just some of them.

Bear in mind that your online reputation remains forever. If somebody writes something negative or unfavorable about you online, it may create a serious disadvantage to you for a long time. It creates more damage if you are not even aware that such thing is lurking in the net. You may never learn the reason behind not getting that apartment that you wanted so much, or why a sure job offer never materialized in the end after painstakingly going through an exceptional interview.

It is important to keep notes or tabs on the things that people say about you in the internet and then take the necessary measure to correct any inaccuracies in the information being distributed.

The Merging of Online and Offline

In this modern era, the online world and activities in real life are becoming more entangled. Most people rely on the internet to shop, make business transactions, get in touch with someone, make a research, find a mate, find some work, and everything else. The modern gadgets, like smartphones and tablets, make it possible to go online wherever you may be and at any given time.

You can do a lot of things online and most people find it convenient and easy. If you are a member of social networking sites, people will be able to find you without delay and get in touch with you. Whenever you go online, you leave a mark that can be positive or negative.

Are you one of those people who rely on the net (Facebook to be precise) to search for an old friend? There's a huge possibility that someone is already tracking you down or searching for you with some help from the internet. Common reasons for such action include:

- Former colleagues or classmates looking for someone to recruit or a partner for a certain business venture.

- Past flames and current partner who are curious about how you are doing and what you did before.

- Children who want to know more about their parents regarding their lives before or whether they were or currently a part of some secret society.

- Property owners who are trying to investigate or look for prospective tenants.

- Employers who are conducting a background research on an aspirant.

- Marketing companies that work with products, services and even political campaigns.

When a modern people needs some information on a particular subject, he relies on internet to give him some answers. Consider the following:

- According to Edelman Insights, two out of three people regard internet as the most reliable provider of information regarding a certain company, organization, or individual.

- Cross-Tab, a business research market firm, revealed that more than half of hiring managers may reject certain candidate due to something they uncovered in the internet about the party involved.

- Most people today make sure to read the online reviews regarding a certain company or product before they try it out.

The things that happen online will surely affect the lives of many people, including you. So, no matter what kind of life you lead, the net has a good quantity of information about you. It would be difficult to deny something that people can read or see online. If you believe that you don't need to control or manage your online presence, you better think again.

Chapter 3: The Need for ORM – Why Online Reputation is Important

It is somewhat foolish to think that negative issues about you in the internet would disappear in time and you don't need to think of ways to quash them completely. Sadly, even when you try to wish so hard for the negative issues to disappear, they will keep lurking the net and someone will be stumbling upon them. The best way to make them go away is to deal with them right from the start.

The negative issues were caused by humans and the technology had nothing to do with the problem. Search engines, like Google, can only yield the result or information that a net surfer asked for. It will give all the information associated with the subject being asked, including negative reviews, conspiracy stories, and juicy gossips.

If people keep clicking and interacting with the negative result, the more search engines will be prompt to show them. So if a link has a catchy title, or if you keep clicking on it everyday, odds are not on your side.

The Chief Importance

Online reputation management won't be able to stop the already published rumors or negative publicity and reviews from circulating, but it can help suppress the unfavorable effects. One way to do it is to make the appalling or dreadful content become less prominent by publishing more important matters.

People love to gossip and one of the ways to kill it is to make people more interested on the fascinating facts about the brand or person. But, make sure not to go overboard. Don't create false impression or twist the truth just to make things more interesting. Understand that it would be hard to defeat human nature, especially when it comes to spreading or picking rumor. You got to admit that even you are more interested on a certain celebrity's scandal than the latest film he/she is in.

Publishing fascinating, positive facts about a brand, company, or person to keep the online communities away from destructive rumors may be quite challenging. It may be even more challenging to convince your client with reputations issues to try to create positive viral content as they may be afraid to fire back. However, professional online reputation management will see to it that everything gets done efficiently and effectively.

Necessity and Benefits

An organization, group, or individual with online presence must keep a positive image or reputation all the time despite having negative reviews. They need to make sure that the positive reviews outweigh the negative ones. Online reputation management can help keep their reputation intact and keep it from plummeting. Of course, there's a need for efficient and effective plan to carry it out. It should be monitored constantly, and regular maintenance is needed to prevent unnecessary trouble. As always, prevention is always the best remedy.

It doesn't matter whether the business is large or small, or whether the individual is already famous or a newcomer. Each entity should not dare overlook the possible benefits and pitfalls that may come their way and should always be ready to counter any attack. The best thing you can do right now is learn more about reputation management online and the things that it can give to help you grow your business.

Having a good reputation can give you power and insurmountable amount of confidence to take a chance and participate in a highly competitive market. Treat your online reputation management as a sort of intangible asset, which can help you attain your goal.

You Need Online Reputation Management

People in this modern time turn to different online platforms (like forums) and social networking sites to get their thoughts known, seek for the information they need, or search for fitting solution to their problem. Conducting survey online and offline to know the people's view regarding a certain topic can be considered outdated.

If you want to know the public's sentiment regarding a certain brand, all you need to do is surf the net and search for the information you need. All the things that you want to know about the brand or company will appear on your list and you just need to click on the specific information that you are looking for. You may also see some negative feedback regarding the product or company.

You need online reputation management to:

1. Improve Sales or Income

We do business with people we trust. And in today's world everyone depends on the internet to gather information. When presented with some problems, the initial reaction of a person is search the net for possible solutions. It is impossible for most us to get on with our lives without internet.

A wise business owner should be able to anticipate the things that his/her customers are looking for when searching the net. You need to make sure that the people you are trying to reach are getting the right kind of message. If you notice that your sales start to drop or continuously fail to reach the target income, you need to investigate immediately. Remember that one of the tasks of online reputation management is to provide the right information to the ones seeking for it.

The initial reaction of some businesspeople when such thing occurs is to discontinue selling the products or services that don't give them profits. On the contrary, it is possible that your customers and potential patrons are not getting the right information they need. It is also possible that they did not get the message that you conveyed.

2. Create a Brand Image

Online reputation management can help you create the appropriate image for the things you offer. You need to be mindful of your brand's image if you want to attain your goal. It is important to establish a good image for your brand and make sure that people will find the right material when they search for it on the net.

Monitoring the responses to all forms of online communication all the time can help you create the perfect brand image. You need to incorporate the image you want your brand to assume to your customers' expectations. Monitor the different reactions of your customers when you post something about your brand in the social media. You need to make necessary adjustments according to the responses you get. Your goal is to gather more positive reactions on your next post.

You need to check the specific aspect of your product that customers appreciate the most or get lots of positive comments. You can make that certain aspect as a focal point of your communication. Take note that the chances of getting it right and wrong are the same when you communicate your brand online. Make the facts straight and don't forget to highlight the things that received positive recognition from the customers.

3. Make them See Your Best Side

When you offer something, everyone tends to search for you online. General public, potential business partners, banks, suppliers, and others are searching for you. The question is would they find you? Conveying the right message and giving out the information that these people need to find come into play.

You need to effectively determine the keywords that people looking for you might type in the search bar, so they can easily find the information that they want to find and make sure to pin it down. The message must be loud and clear, so they won't forget you. Keep in mind that there are businesspeople that also offer products or services like yours. It is imperative to make your searchers see your best side and decide not to look further when they find you.

Most people base their final decision on the available information that they come across. If they are satisfied with the information they get about you, most of them won't look further because they already found what they need. If you offer all the information they need but your negative reputation is smacking them on their faces, don't expect them to stick around and give you a chance. You won't surely do some business with someone with a negative reputation, why should they?

4. Gain the Trust of Your Customers and Make Yourself Credible

To attain success, it is important for a business to have loyal customers who put their unyielding trust in your brand and who are willing to spread the word about your business. Your customers can provide you with an honest-to-goodness advertisement because they share their personal experience with your product along with their sentiments. Your customer may narrate them to their friends and family or post it in their social media. It's deeper than having a good product or service - it's about your passion, your commitment, your ideology to create a better world by providing something valuable and that ends up creating a good product and service. For this hard work and empathy with your values, people follow, trust your work and do business with you.

Sell a good product that has a surprise to mesmerize them, go the extra mile and they will love you because everybody loves to brag about a good deal.

As you get more positive reviews and encouragement from your customers, you also build your credibility. Other people who come across your brand and find that many people post good reviews may want to know more about it. Make sure that when interested customers search for additional information about your brand they will find the data they need. Online reputation management can help you show potential clients your best side and convince them that you are being truthful with the things you present.

5. Find the most Suitable Individuals to Work with

The success of your business also depends on the professionalism, passion, diligence, dedication, and work ethics of the people you employ. The best candidates are often hard to come by. Like you, they also look for the most suitable work place for them and will naturally seek for a company with good reputation.

When potential employees read your positive reviews and establish that your company has good reputation, they might just give your company a try. You can also try searching for that candidate's reputation online and see if he/she is the one that fits in your company. When all is well and good between the two of you, look forward to a harmonious working relationship. It is also advisable that the candidate also fits in with the rest of the team. You need to keep your entire team happy and satisfied to get things done smoothly and on time.

Hire a Company, Professional or Do It Yourself

You can handle your own online reputation management or hire someone to do it for you. This book can guide you on how to do it and you need to devote some of your time learning it. Understand that online reputation management is a continuing process. If you want to do it on your own, you need to especially dedicate some hours for it. You need to squeeze it in your busy schedule if you don't want it to fail.

Now, before you decide to do your own online reputation management you need to determine efficiency and efficacy of your action. You need to ask yourself, is it wise to undertake the task using your own ability? You also need to consider if it's more cost effective to just hire a company or professional and dedicate your time serving your customers and minding your business.

Online reputation management is important, and it must be done continuously (not just when you feel like checking it) to ensure that nothing goes wrong.

Chapter 4: Online Reputation Management (ORM) vs. Search Engine Optimization (SEO)

You already know that ORM and SEO go hand in hand. It is true that ORM and SEO share some similarities as well as differences.

SEO focuses more on landing a specific page or website on the top of the list of search results to attract more attention. Its main concern is to rank a certain website or web page. ORM, on the hand, focuses more on manipulating the collection of websites that appear together with your site or brand in the search results. Their measures of success and tactics are not the same.

Talk About Multiple Targets

In SEO campaign, you commonly aim to get a certain page occupy one of the top positions in the search results. If you can get a certain page to occupy the first rank, you can get the most benefits and advantages. In ORM, it does not matter if a certain site occupies the first or the seventh position. The primary concern of ORM is to control the content of the first page. The ORM techniques are created to build materials ecosystem of related stories that are different from one another but complements each other.

Choice of Keywords

SEO gives utmost importance to keywords and it typically aims for a group of connected keywords or terms with the objective of getting the attention of site visitors from numerous searches. For example, a local carpet cleaning business in Los Angeles may target keywords like "Los Angeles carpet cleaner" and "carpet cleaning in Jacksonville".

When you do online reputation management campaign, you need to target specific search terms that can create an impact to your reputation. It is not the goal of ORM to attract so many visitors. Its main concern is to present the relevant information that searchers need no matter which site they prefer to visit.

Promotion vs. Displacement

The main objective of SEO is move a specific site to the top of search results. Take Amazon as an example. Amazon tries its best to make people click on their site and not their competitor's site. They tried their best to make their website occupy a high rank.

ORM, on the other hand, tries to move down a particular site. It aims to displace ambiguous information or rumor with the help of materials with top quality. It doesn't matter whether your searchers click on your Facebook account, LinkedIn profile, search queries on popular sites or business website as long as they don't click on the link where a disgruntled employee's tirade is posted.

Making SEO Works for You

Let us briefly discuss how you can make SEO help you with your ORM, especially when it comes to local search. Later, you will appreciate this brief discussion more when you are on the chapter regarding the ultimate guide to good online image.

Here's a scenario: you are new in a certain area or you've just moved in and you don't know anyone around, but you need to establish your presence in the neighborhood, what would you do? There's really one simple thing you can do and that is to introduce yourself and make others take notice of you. If there's community event, participate in it. Be a volunteer in a certain community drive and meet more people. You can tell them something about you and where you live so they can easily find you when they need something.

The scenario above is similar to something that requires collaboration of ORM and SEO. The ORM part is when you try to win the good side of the people you meet and make them realize your positive side. The SEO part is targeting the local area to establish your presence and specifying your exact location with a plan of dominating the area.

Local search marketing is about targeting geo-specific and industry-specific terms. For example, a restaurant may have various locations within New Orleans. When planning for optimization strategy, the first thing to do is look for some geo-specific keywords + restaurant to see the number of times people search for them. You can use Google AdWords Keyword Tool, Google Trends or Kwfinder for example.

You will see that a certain location is searched more than the other. You will also see other suggestions as well as the estimated monthly search rate for the suggested phrases.

If you want to get more keyword ideas, you can also type in the keyword you have in mind in Google search bar. Scroll down to view all searches that are related to your keyword.

Chapter 5: ORM General Rules and Tools that can Help You Monitor Your Online Image

Depending on your requirements, online reputation management can be multifaceted and long-winded or relatively straightforward. Most campaigns of ORM follow general rules as guide, and it is advisable not to shy away from them. Always keep them in mind, especially if you have decided to handle your own ORM.

Remember that Algorithm Generates Search Results

Computers automatically run complex calculations to determine your online reputation. It would be too much work for someone to take time and gather all the information that can help verify the things that the public find interesting. Social media sites and search engines create sophisticated deductions regarding the things that the public find appealing or would like to know more about.

Popularity Over Accurateness of Information

The algorithm cannot tell whether the information about you is accurate or not. Popularity of the information where you are involved becomes the algorithm's main gauge. Expect to have a negative online reputation when a lawsuit that had been dismissed some years back or embarrassing photos (both can harm your online reputation), and other intrigues about you are more popular than the information regarding your good side. The best way to counter the nasty information is publish relevant, high quality materials that your searchers hope to find in the net.

Don't Always Check and Click

It is annoying to learn that there are web pages that contain defaming content about you, and it is tempting to visit them repeatedly – don't do that. Each time you click on the link, you are actually helping those nasty web pages rank faster than usual. The search engines will also treat it as something relevant to you. When the negative web pages occupy the top spots on the search results and people try to look for you in the net, the first things they will see are those pages. It is almost impossible for your searchers not to click on the link and when they do they will see the things that you don't want them to know.

For your safety and to make those pages practically disappear, don't click on the links. Tell your friends and family not to visit those pages and explain the consequences when they do. Not offering an explanation after you've prohibited them from clicking on the link will only raise their curiosity and will naturally visit the abominable pages.

Later, you will learn how you can eliminate negative search results.

Don't Waste Your Precious Time with Detractors

If someone posted something unfavorable in a certain forum about you, don't add a comment, retort by writing something offensive, and avoid referring the unflattering material in forums. Doing so can prevent sending unnecessary attention to the posted material. The number of views will stop or lessen, and eventually it will die naturally. Put your energy to your online reputation management and your business instead of wasting time with detractors. However, it is different when it comes to reviews.

Finally, always remember the golden rule of social media: be positive or be silent.

If you face fake news and cyberbullying, report the behavior to the website. Do not keep engaging raging comments and dislike as they are social signals that can boost the page even more.

Let Your Story be Known

You need a sturdy support of accurate, positive content to boost your reputation within the online communities. You can only promote the things that are already exposed, and you need to let people know more about your good side. To do this, you can post some of your videos on YouTube, start a blog, and others. You may also need a team that can help you promote or boost your positive side to affect search results.

Harness the Power of Social Media

Do you have many connections in LinkedIn? It is important to keep an updated resume because you'll never know when a potential client or business partner is interested to transact with you. Do you own a Twitter account? It is best that you have one and when you sign up you can have your full name as user name or handle.

Social media sites often provide a good ranking in search results. Moreover, you can choose and monitor the content that you want it to show. Social media sites can bring a huge difference (in a favorable way) to your image.

Be Cautious of Your Privacy

You need to be careful with your personal information that you post online. It is best to opt out of services that can easily divulge your personal matters online and delete your information on sites that search for people. Cyber criminals or hackers can use your personal data to do something unscrupulous and affect your reputation as well.

Think that Everything is Forever

If something related to you is published online, it permanently becomes part of your online presence or image. The published content will continue to rank as long as someone clicks on it. The search results are not chronologically arranged and that means outdated information and old news or stories about you continue to exist. The search engines will continue to treat them as information related to you. This can actually put you in favorable and unfavorable situations. You must be really careful when posting something online.

Tools that can Help You Monitor your Brand

There are a lot of available tools that can help you monitor the online presence of your brand. Use them and gain immense benefits.

1. Google Alerts

Google is one of the best friends that you can rely on in this life. It is especially dependable when you need to monitor your brand online. It would be easy for you to track results from different groups, video results, blogs, news, and your web or online presence. According to 'Nuff', Google Alert is your best choice for brand mentions.

2. Social Mention

Google Alerts has a version in social media called Social Mention. It can help you keep track of your brand in various social platforms around the web. You are allowed to download the Excel file, receive email alerts, or you can choose to have a feed subscription.

3. Twitter Search

Over the years, Twitter has become one of the best places promote and keep an eye on your brand's online presence. Almost everybody with Twitter account re-tweets content regardless if they use a hashtag or not. Twitter search allows you to organize your search parameters such as Twitter account, sentiment, location, links, dates, and others.

4. Yahoo Alerts

You can set-up Yahoo Alerts for free and you can track feeds, local news, stocks, and more. You can also monitor news by keyword, which provides ease and convenience plus you can save time. You can get notifications through Yahoo Messenger, mobile, or email.

5. Go Fish Digital Complaint Search

Complaint Search Box allows you to look for negative reviews on more than 40 complaint websites using Google search engine. It is a free service that's quick and easy to use. You can do daily searches to check if there are customers that having negative experience with your brand or your business.

You will be able to monitor the things that your customers might be saying about you or your brand. You need to check from time to time to see if something new has popped up. Go Fish Digital also offers paid services for online reputation management.

6. Hootsuite

This social media management tool can help take care all of your social media accounts in the same place. It would be easy for you to listen and associate with the people who follow you, arrange future messages, and take hold of through social media analytics so you'll know how people perceive your content. You can necessary adjustments or improvements when called for.

The free service includes basic analytics report, program messages, and hook up three social profiles. You can also make an upgrade by paying $10 per month and you will get way more than the basic offer.

7. Naymz

Naymz can help you manage and monitor (or trace) your social impact, which is closely linked to your online image. If you have high social influence, expect your online reputation to rise.

Naymz has a program that's called RepScore, which can rate your online influence in various social networks and relatively compare it to other account holders from the same social network. It has the ability to assess how you appear in the eyes of your peers. Would they listen and associate with you? Do they think you are unique, in a good way, and holds great value as an influencer? It gives a score between 1 and 99, with 1 being the worst.

8. Yex

If you want something that can help you supervise your online listings on review sites and location, Yex is the one you should visit. It can help you verify whether the posted information is correct.

It has PowerListings tool that points out the error rate of the posted information, so you can make the necessary corrections and ensure that your customers will reach you. The program needs you to enter your zip code, business address, contact number, and business name before it skims through the local review sites and listing in its database.

9. Talkwalker

Talkwalker offers its social search for free and it helps you see the public's sentiment towards your services, products, or brand during the last seven days. It helps you recognize the articles, tweets, and posts that lead to social discussion regarding your company or brand.

Talkwalker's data coverage spans over 150 million websites, including social networks. Expect to get a complete view of your brand's reputation across forums, blogs, web news, social media, and others. You can have as many searches as you want and have the results in seconds. You can conduct a real-time online reputation monitoring.

Talkwalker Alerts is a simple alternative to Google Alerts. It can immediately notify you whenever it detects that your keyword comes up on the net.

To create an alert, enter the keyword you want to track (could be your name, company, products, services, or brand). You also need to include the frequency, language, and media type. Don't forget to add your email address.

10. Image Raider

Image Raider is a somewhat straightforward tool that is keen on monitoring possible misuse of your images. You only need to upload an image that is associated or linked to you into the Image Raider. It will immediately track down all uses of the uploaded image across Yandex, Bing, and Google.

The ones who usually avail of Image Raider's services are: people who want to know the image's original location or source, individuals who suspect that someone used their images or photos online, photographers and rights owners hunting for websites that used their photos without permission, and digital marketers or SEOs.

11. Yotpo

Yotpo is different from most tools that help you monitor your brand. Yotpo focuses more on helping you enhance your reputation by encouraging customers to give and post positive reviews regarding your brand.

It comes in free and paid versions. For the free service, you can develop a customizable review widget, automatically send requests for review after a customer purchased the product and generate emails that contain review requests. For the paid service, you get much more than the free service, including instagram social curation, reviews via campaigns in social media, and more.

There are more tools out there and many of them come with a fee. If you think that that a certain paid tool can help you a lot and won't affect your operation cost, you can go ahead and avail its services.

Let the general rules guide you when you monitor your online reputation and let the tools help you achieve your goal.

Chapter 6: Things You Need to Understand About Online Reputation Managers

Many people use their social media accounts to get connected with friends and loved ones, share some good things (and some bad things) that happened to them, and gossip. Some people post photos, update their status, post some comments, and share whatever it is they find that's worth sharing. People do not mind even if they don't get any benefits from sharing something. They just want to share or use their social account as they please. Everyone who owns an account in different social networking sites should change the way he/she looks at the said online communities. A social networking site is more than just a place to socialize and meet new friends online.

In the Eyes of the Employers

For many companies or employers who are looking for someone to hire, the applicant's social media profile could give them some idea about the candidate. Many recruiters turn to social media if they want to see a candidate's comprehensive information that cover letter and simple resume may not be able to provide. Depending on what the employer looks for in a potential employee, the applicant's online reputation can make or break an employment contract.

In today's competitive market, a strong online presence is a plus factor in the eyes of an employer. Companies looking for a suitable employee to hire usually rely on the net to know more about a certain candidate. The Creative Group, a marketing and staffing agency, said that they are likely to rely on the internet to give them some information about a certain applicant that caught their interest. If they find the candidate's online content impressive (like commentary that's thought-provoking), they may likely set the time to interview the applicant. Negative remarks can diminish the interest of a hiring manager to consider the applicant for the position that he/she tries to land.

The survey conducted by The Creative Group revealed the following:

- 68% of executives are likely to review the LinkedIn profiles of applicants.

- 65% of executives use the applicant's name to search for information about him/her online.

- 46% would visit the applicant's Facebook pages and check them out.

-1/3 of executives may want to review the Twitter profiles of candidates.

- 29% would scrutinize the candidate's blog posts.

When the recruiting team wants to know the creative style and other projects of a certain candidate, they may likely visit the applicant's Instagram and online portfolios.

The most common mistakes that candidates and professionals make with regards to their online profiles are:

- Not making regular updates.

- Revealing too much information.

It is advisable to update the social media profiles regularly and control the information being shared in the online communities.

About Professional Online Reputation Managers

Employers looking for the most suitable employees rely on the net to give them some background information on the applicants that caught their interest. If employers check the applicant's online reputation, other people do that too when they need to find out more about a certain brand and the group or person behind it. In this modern day and age, everyone should think of ways in keeping the online reputation positive.

As you try to maintain your online reputation positive, a competitor or someone who holds a grudge against you may do everything in his/her power to bring you down. Your "enemy" will surely find new things to bring your online reputation down and even create some obstacles for you.

1. If you have a business or want to create a good reputation for your brand, you may need to consider hiring a professional online reputation manager.

If you have a booming business, expect competitors to find ways to eliminate you in the race. You may want to consider hiring an online reputation manager to manage your online presence on your behalf.

The best professional online reputation managers are part tech experts and part PR gurus. Their field of specialization is giving online makeovers. They usually do that by practically annihilating negative search results and promoting content that highlights the image that their client wants to own.

There are online reputation managers that have clients from Fortune 500 companies, moms and dads, and others. The professionals can help their clients gain possible maximum control on the things that people see or read about them in the internet. The information that they may control could be the things that they want people to learn about them or materials that they don't want others to know, such as a medical record.

2. If it's impossible for you to manage your digital reputation, it is best to let someone do it for you.

The internet has brought us a lot of good things and lately there are lots of not-so-good things practically pop up every minute. The reputation that you've so tried hard to establish may suddenly get tarnished under the manipulative hands of unknown people. They could be your competitors, detractors, or those who just want to make things difficult for you. It is also possible that someone hired them to give you trouble, and they could be anywhere in the planet.

Unfavorable or bad things that happened in your past (that were supposed to be buried with time) may suddenly become things that haunt your present as well as your future when someone dug them up. Your bad past can become a threat. You must quash the negative facts and rumors before they create havoc in your life. Control them before they control your future. Contracting someone to manage your digital reputation can help you a lot in your current and future endeavors.

Your rising popularity could be the reason for the emergence of the bad things in your past. Your unknown enemy could be using someone to do the dirty work for them, and you need to fight fire with fire. By keeping a positive online presence with relevant content useful resources, you can overcome the negative presence. Plus, you can use SEO techniques on these new articles to help boost their ranking surpassing the negative ones.

3. You can choose to manage your own online reputation, but it is advisable to let a professional do it for you. The best professionals are able to use SEO techniques together with compelling content. And the best teams even have PRs to help create positive content on reputable media sites.

You should be aware by now that there are hackers that can easily breach your computer system and cyber security, especially if you don't have reliable software that can safeguard your online presence and network. These hackers or cyber offenders typically use viruses and malware to infiltrate your network or computer system. If you don't have a reliable system security, the hacker can easily gain access to your personal data and other things that you want to protect.

As mentioned earlier, professional online reputation managers are also tech savvy. They will be able to detect if your computer system or network has been breached and employ necessary measure to prevent your online reputation from plummeting. They can also help you protect your system against any infiltration attempt from hackers. They also enhance your digital presence while giving you the protection you need.

There are things that you can also do on your own to boost your online reputation. You can create a well-curated, pensive LinkedIn profile. You can use your real name as your handle name or something relevant to your line of work. Keep your social media accounts updated.

4. An online reputation manager can help you understand the importance of having good online reputation.

Your attackers can be vicious and unforgiving when it comes to damaging your online image. Understand that your ruined reputation can also affect the way people view the individuals that are connected to you. It will affect your loved ones, friends, and business partners.

In this modern world, people can destroy you completely without using brute force. We are in the digital age and only the cunning individuals can survive. Your online reputation manager can point out the things that are at stake and design a plan to protect your reputation and boost it at the same time. You need to be clear on the things that you want to achieve and the kind of image that you want the online community to remember when they think of you or immediately associate a certain image to you.

Whether or not you are selling or offering something to the public, you need to keep a good online reputation. You will never know when you can use it to gain benefits and advantages. No matter how you look at it, having a good online reputation is still better than having negative publicity.

5. Online reputation managers don't seek to erase negative content about you online.

Professional online reputation managers are not really capable of erasing a content that's already a part of the net. Even a lawsuit won't be able to take it down. The good news is that if it does not appear on the first page of the search list, it is practically non-existent. Over time, the negative content will eventually fall behind even more until no one remembers its existence. Just make sure not to click on the link.

Be Careful of People Who Promise to Erase Negative Content

Any published information becomes a public domain. Even if the piece of information is something negative about you, it is impossible to retract it from the public's view once published.

You may encounter an individual or group that may offer to erase the negative content if you pay a certain fee. Would you close a deal with such individual? To blunt, you are taking a great risk if you do that. They may use unscrupulous means to keep the negative content practically invisible like hacking websites and people's accounts. That person may only extort more money from you to keep the content offline.

For all you know, the person who approached you could be someone who published the demeaning content in the first place. You will actually lose more money eventually if you give in to his demands. An online reputation manager, on the other hand, can help you make the negative content practically disappear and also enhance your online reputation, which the extortionist wouldn't do even if you pay him a handsome amount of money.

If you need an online reputation makeover, only a professional online reputation manager can help you.

Chapter 7: Simple ORM for the Unsophisticated Net User

If you want to manage your online reputation, you only need to remember few important tips. Take note that the tips are just basic steps. The more technical aspects are not included. You may need to hire someone to do that for you. If you can write your own content, you may do so and make sure that you will be able to get your message across.

If you suck at writing a good material or content, you better let someone handle it for you. You can pay someone to write your content for you and the price for such service is usually competitive. There are lots of online writing services that you can choose from. You can do your research first and see what their clients say about them. You need to find a reliable service provider with good reputation and online presence.

The author of an online reputation management book once tagged a funny anecdote about hiding a dead body on the second page of Google search results as a geek joke. This only implies that the negative content about you or your brand found on the second page of the Google search results can be considered dead and non-existent. It won't do any harm to your online reputation anymore.

The succeeding sections are the tips that an unsophisticated should consider when managing his/her online image.

Tip #1: Search for Your Brand or Name on the Net

Type your name or your brand on search engines and social media search bar and press enter. Do the same in Google images. Inspect the search list and see if you can find something negative about you or your brand. It is advisable to set up your own Google Alert, so you can monitor if there's a new content. You can choose to have the notifications emailed to you just once on each day to prevent your inbox from receiving too much.

Now, try searching for yourself on other search engines and what do you see? Don't just rely on Google when you are managing your online reputation. People tend to use different search engines when they want to find out more about certain brand, personality, company, or organization. Find out all the things, good and bad being said regarding your brand or you in general.

When you search for yourself, search for your full name, possible misspellings of your name, related keywords to your reputation, birth name (for ladies), nicknames, and even your moniker if you have one. You may also include your occupation, name of the university or college that you had attended or currently attending, or hometown. If you are worried about what your potential business partner or boss might discover, it is best to search for identifiable information that any person may gain access to, such as phone number, username that you habitually use, or your email address.

It is also advisable to comb through the forums and blogs that you always visit or join in the discussions as well as social media accounts. You need to check if you have no derogatory photos or posts that may affect your image and ruin your chance of having a promising business partnership or career. Now that you have known this, stay away from posting damning comments and sharing indecent or inappropriate photos in the internet because they may ruin your online reputation. Delete the social media accounts that you think may affect your image and those that you no longer use. You can go to Wayback Machine to check if any of the accounts that you already deleted are still in cache form.

You may also need to check the forum posts, blogs, and social media accounts of your friends and loved ones just to make sure that you won't get implicated by their actions. You may not be able to reverse or delete the things that were already posted, but you can prepare something that can help you counter the possible effect of the said posts on your reputation when time comes. Your detractors or competitors will dig and do everything to bring you down, including using the derogatory posts that your friends and loved ones had made.

Tip #2: Adjust Your Privacy Setting on Your Social Media Accounts

If you can't part with your social media accounts that contain so many things that you can only dare share with people who are close to you (such as embarrassing photos and comments that you don't want your potential employer or business partner to see), you can change your privacy setting. You need to scour the net to check the links of those embarrassing photos and comments that you made on your own blog. Try to remove them as much as possible or make them private.

Go to privacy settings and tools page of the social media account that you don't want others to know and make the necessary adjustments. However, your detractors or stalkers as well as possible employers and business partners are quite clever. Keeping your social accounts private might be insufficient. It is best to delete photos that may ruin your image form your social media account or ask the person who shared it online to remove it. Don't just untag yourself because the photo will remain visible and you cannot be certain that the persons you don't want it to see won't have any access to it.

You can also ask Google to delete your private information from the search results, click this link to redirect you to the site. However, such action is not applicable to emotional blog posts or pictures.

Tip #3: Place Your Content in a Many Locations

There are numerous sites (like About.me, WordPress, and Tumbler) that allow you to post blog articles. Keep your content fresh, relevant, positive and viral.

Tip #4: Be a Part of Social Networks

You can get enough exposure if you are a part of social networks. If you feel like you can't spare some time to actively participate in the discussions or happenings in the different social networks, you still can still join them. Spare some time to complete the needed details in your profile so people can check you out and follow the latest news around you.

There different social media sites and it is advisable to have an account from the major sites or any site that appears to be promising. You will never know when the lesser sites of today might become the most popular tomorrow. You are not required to be too involved, but it is important not be dormant. You need to provide regular updates to alert your followers and customers. It is recommended to provide fresh content at least once a month to keep your visitors and customers in touch.

Tip #5: Try Your Best to Make Your Presence Known on Your Chosen Social Media Sites

It is important to optimize your presence and customizing the URL of your social media accounts can help you a lot. You can repeat your name in the URL and make sure that you do it in an appropriate and effective manner. For example, if you have an account in LinkedIn (it is strongly recommended to have one) you can go to your profile page, look for "public profile" and edit your URL. Instead of having this long URL:

http://www.linkedin.com/profile/view?id=302699458&locale=en_US&trk=uyah

You can customize it to something like this:

http://www.linkedin.com/in/reneesmith

As you can see, the name of the person who owns the profile is reflected on the URL. It is also advisable to use your full name instead of nickname or an alias. You can also link your other social media sites if you have such option in your account. It enhances your online presence even more.

If there are many people who have the same name as yours, then you may want to change it a bit without losing your name's professionalism. You need to change it to distinguish yourself from the people that share the same name. You can add your middle name if you want. This is to ensure that your customers, potential employers or business partners, and other group or people who are interested with the things you offer will surely find you and not some imposter. This will also deter those who want to create trouble for you by using your name when posting something defamatory.

To separate your private life from your professional life in the net, you might want to consider changing the name in your social media account that you use to share and communicate with friends and loved ones. You can use any name as long as it won't coincide with the information in the social media account that you use for your profession.

Tip #6: Keep Private Things Truly Private

To be blunt, nothing is truly private when you post or share something in your social media account even if you keep things private. You already have an idea about the cyber criminals called hackers and they can always find ways to expose your deepest, darkest secrets whenever they want. As long as you have photos and other things that you keep in your social media account, blog, or website, they will be able to dig it up and expose you to their hearts' content.

The best thing to do to avoid seeing yourself in such situation is not to keep such photos in your online accounts and be extremely cautious when posting comments or sentiments over the net. Everything you say or do can bring down your online reputation, and you don't want that to happen. A moment of carelessness could be your downfall.

You also need to be cautious of your actions and make sure not to give your detractors or "enemies" to take a photo of your embarrassing or scandalous moments. Just think that someone is always watching you and hoping that you make an irreparable mistake or damaging action, so they can deal with you finally.

Tip #7: Create Your Brand

Most of the time, suppressing your past can tire you out. Instead of thinking and planning for your future, you can't move forward because you are busy trying to erase your past that may affect your reputation. If you already did the best you could in erasing your embarrassing past in the world of internet, it's time to stop and begin focusing on your future. You might want to start building your brand and your future.

First, you need to build your professional identity to give your brand a more trustworthy background. You can choose to have new social network accounts, which must be strictly for professional use to avoid inappropriate posts from people who do not seriously take your desire to have a good online reputation. You can create new forum posts, blog posts, and articles that can help boost your reputation.

Here are the simple steps to help you start building your brand:

1. Start a blog or your own website.

Start with a simple website or blog to get the ball rolling. You don't need a professional website or blog, but at least make sure that it's good enough to impress. Post regularly on your blog and the content should be helpful and relevant to your brand and the image that you want people to remember about you or the things you offer.

You can also purchase a domain name. Different experts have varying opinions about the amount of effort and money that you need to put into buying domain name. The co-founder and CEO of BrandYourself recommended grabbing a number of domain names. He said that the more domain name you have, the better. However, some experts say that it is rather excessive and seems impractical.

You can try keeping one domain name and exert a bit more effort to write high quality content that you will put on your site. You can also write your short bio and post it on your site. Include a story from your life that might inspire others or make them look at you favorably. You can also include your curriculum vitae, which must be honest and simple. It won't hurt if you make it look impressive, but don't tell lies in an attempt to elevate your status. People will find out and your reputation gets affected.

2. Don't forget to join different social networks.

Aside from the previously discussed social media accounts that you need to have, you can also join review sites like Amazon and Yelp. Don't forget to create separate accounts for your social and professional online life.

3. Become the expert that everyone looks up to.

Being an expert in your field can make you earn the trust of most people. People don't easily believe anyone's statement or explanation, unless the one speaking or explaining is an expert. Try to make your name appear on industry magazines or publications to build your credibility. You can coordinate with sites like Media Diplomat and HARO (Help A Reporter Out), which bring reporters and sources together. You can be the expert as a source.

You can appear like an expert in your field if you try to place yourself as one via social media, video blogs, forum posts, or blog posts.

After creating a good background for the brand that you want to build, everything that follows should go smoothly. There may be little bumps along the way, but you should be able to handle them.

Tip #8: Remain Vigilant and Diplomatic

You need to remain vigilant all the time if you want to keep a positive reputation all the time. Use the tools that can help you monitor new web content or information about your company, brand, or you.

There are negative comments or posts that can make your blood boil, but you need to remain calm and diplomatic. Having a word war with your detractors can only bring negative impact on your online reputation. Most of the time, your detractors do that on purpose to make you angry and drive you to do things that can bring harm to you and your brand as well as your entire business operation.

Your vigilance and diplomacy can help you hinder any attempt of your detractors to bring you down.

Important Reminders that You Need to Keep in Mind

There are certain things that you need to keep in mind, so you can manage your online reputation well.

1. Always give importance to online reviews.

Prudent customers always check the reviews on the product or services that they plan to buy. They want to make sure that they will be getting their money's worth. It has been customary to view at least three to five brands of the same product and see which one is really worth it. SEO tactics can help a lot in ranking the brand in the search list, but customers rely more on online reviews. They usually take the top brands into consideration (based on their ranking on the search list), but the brand that gets chosen in the end is usually the one that has the most number of positive reviews.

2. Refrain from posting fake reviews.

There are business owners that post fake positive reviews to boost their brand's ranking. Don't post fake reviews or hire someone to post fake reviews. You may enjoy the attention now, but not for long. Customers reading a lot of positive reviews for your brand will naturally have high expectations that your products are really good, almost perfect. They will no longer to hesitate to buy your product and try it. When it failed to meet their expectations, negative reviews will surely pour like rain.

There will always be a group of customers that won't be satisfied with your product. If you let some negative reviews to appear, your customers may still buy it but they won't expect too much from your product.

3. Be tactical when you ask for feedback.

You can encourage your customers to give appropriate feedback regarding the things you offer, but make sure to ask from ones you can trust. Your detractors may pose as your customers and the feedback they will give you won't be reliable. You ask for feedback to improve what needs improvement in your brand and you can only do that if you ask those who can give you an honest assessment.

4. Create a feedback routine with easy to understand instruction.

When asking for a feedback, you are actually asking for a favor from your trusted customers. Don't make them answer a series of questions like they are taking their finals. Don't give ambiguous instructions that they will have some hard time to decipher. Make it simple, quick, and easy. It should not take them more than two to five minutes to answer any question or sample something.

5. When posting their review, make sure that your customers include the item or service that they used.

Remind your customers to include the product or service that they use when they create their review. It will serve as guide to the ones reading it so they'll know the specific item or service that the reviewing customer find satisfactory or needs improvement.

6. Gather the customer reviews first.

Go to your website and gather the customer reviews before you show them to the online community. You don't want to post fake or all positive reviews, but it doesn't mean you must post all the negative reviews as well. Your detractors will surely post damaging reviews to bring you down and you need to filter those. Posting too many negative reviews can pull down your online reputation. You need time to address the negative reviews before you can allow the rest if the online community see them.

7. Customize your online review funnel.

You need to customize your online review funnel to make it easier and more convenient for your customers when they review your product. The customized review funnel also makes it easier for the readers to go through the review and determine the real worth of your products or services.

8. Do not forget to associate yourself or connect with the reviewers.

It doesn't matter if the review is positive or not, but you should always connect or associate yourself with the people who review your products or services. Be sure to thank the reviewers and encourage those who made positive comments to post more reviews about your brand in the future.

9. Don't worry too much about negative reviews.

It is only natural for a certain product to have its share of negative reviews. Why? It's because not everyone has the same preferences. Brand X may fail to satisfy the requirements of customer A while customer B is pleased with it.

When dealing with negative reviews or comments, respond to them in a professional manner. Avoid waging a word war with the person who made the review or posted a negative comment. Always keep yourself and your brand positive and prompt to fix any bad experience and review your processes. Negative reviews create balance and can help customers from having extremely high expectations from the product.

The things you learned in this chapter can serve as your guide when managing your online reputation.

Chapter 8: You are the Topic of their Discussion

You should know by now that online reputation management is not limited to monitoring your social media accounts. Some people believe that ORM is a bit like public relations – they may be similar in some ways, but they are also entirely different from one another.

It is almost impossible to survive in the competitive arena of the business world if you have bad online presence or negative reputation. People will surely talk about you but not in a good way. That's why it is of utmost importance to have and maintain a good image all the time.

You are their Topic

In the past, companies were not that interested to associate with customers and just sell their products. Customers were passive then and could not express their opinions.

After a few years, things radically changed. Currently, websites no longer serve as static flyers or pamphlets. There is a need for user-generated content. To ensure success, companies need to interact more on social networks. Companies nowadays use the Law of Reciprocity to give content, values, samples, experiences before they ask you to buy it.

Whether it's a small or large business, your clients and most people who search for the things you offer will naturally make you and your business as the topic of their discussion. They may tweet about the latest products or services that you offer. Customers post their experience with your product on Facebook, leave a comment on your website or blog, and much more. Your customers, potential clients, and even detractors actively participate in discussions about your brand.

People make reviews and prefer to voice out their thoughts. Even if you don't own the product that they talk about on the net, but you own the same type of item, you might get pulled into their discussion when they begin to compare it against your brand.

It is good that you can react well to criticisms or negative comments without blowing your top or without sounding like you take much offense. Remember that the best brands are interested in offering the best solution, they are passed behind egos. Showing that you are interested in improving and that you are true to your values, can harvest more followers and liking. Before you react on negative comments, it is best to calm yourself first and don't post what you think right away. You also have an option to remove or not show such comments if you think that it will greatly affect your online reputation even if you give proper explanation in a calm tone.

There are times when you also need to determine carefully whether to react or not. There are seemingly negative comments that don't need your reaction at all. Sometimes your loyal patrons will do that for you. You can let them argue for a while until it dies naturally. In case their word war seems to be getting out of hand and won't be stopping anytime soon, you can choose to cut in and give proper explanation or give them some more time as long as their tirade doesn't affect your good online reputation.

You need to properly weigh things and carefully determine the best time to react or should you make any reaction at all. Giving your reaction too quickly may not be good. On the other hand, giving a late reaction could make you lose more than you can bargain for. That's why it is recommended to constantly monitor your public reputation and not just when you feel like doing it.

If you think that a particular comment must be dealt with immediately, then do so without making things bigger than it is. You need to be careful with your choice of words because your detractors may use them against you. Don't allow them to twist your words and influence the online community to go against you.

You can also rely on social media monitoring to help you gather content from online reviews, tweets, blog posts, and more.

The Risk of being Transparent

Recently, there's a new business commandment came was born and that is to be transparent. It somehow directs the companies to welcome feedback and criticisms from customers and potential clients. Companies that embrace this new form of communication with the public may gain more benefits from it.

But, what does being transparent entail? Here is a list of some examples:

1. A company should not hide the criticisms they receive from their audience. Instead of hiding it, they need to address it in public.

2. A company must ask and welcome feedbacks from the audience.

3. A company must put up a one to one communication channel.

4. Employees of the company must be allowed to discuss the company's product and services in public.

Most businesses that belong to small and medium scales do not spend much time (and money) on communication, and they believe that they need to exert great effort to accomplish it. They usually employ incorrect methods because, for them, the concept is a challenge that they need to overcome, and such thought makes them less enthusiastic to make it work.

Companies are taking great risk for being transparent, but not being transparent could be more perilous eventually.

A Blast on Your Online Reputation

The complaints posted on social networks about you or your product must be addressed properly so it won't get big. Always remember to do it calmly and without losing your sense of propriety even if you think that the complaint seems over the top. However, if your company is currently facing a serious problem, it is best to pour your energy into solving your business dilemma first before you deal with other matters. Compared to your current difficulties, the complaints are considered as less significant matter.

There are negative coverage, hate sites, and off-putting reviews that can affect your sales and online reputation for a long time. They can create severe damage to your business if you don't act quickly. They bring more harm to your reputation and business than mere complaints in social networks because they also pop up in search engine results. Just imagine the consequences when someone Googles your brand and the search results yield numerous derogatory materials about your company or brand.

You need to be wary of:

- Negative Media Coverage

The saying about bad publicity as something that does not exist in this world, according to Phineas T. Barnum. That could only apply to controversial celebrities or personalities that become even more popular as people gossip about them. In many cases, unfavorable online media coverage and content regarding a particular product can negatively affect the brand or company. Many potential customers of the product may choose not to try the brand anymore. Later, even the customers who are used to be loyal to the company may choose to withdraw their support due to the negative publicity that may have also influenced their decision.

- Hate Sites

There are also hate sites that can ruthlessly damage your brand's reputation. Some people dare to go further than posting off-putting remarks or reviews and even develop a website that aims to bring more trouble to the company that owns the brand. The hate sites sometimes directly insult the public figures or companies. They often post false information and illegal content just to crush the involved party's reputation. They are merciless and disregard proper decorum. When a potential customer type something like this on the search bar:

"The truth about [name of company that the searcher is trying to look into]"

or something like this:

"Is [name of the company or brand] a rip off?"

and all sorts of negative materials come out, your potential customer might not even dare take a look at your company's products again. In their minds, the things you offer are nothing but crap.

- Negative Reviews

Too much negative reviews can harm your online reputation. Earlier we already mentioned that you need to balance your positive and negative reviews that customers post on your website. What if they are posted on the sites that you have no authority to control?

There are different online review sites, which allow the users to post their thoughts on your brand. They can freely say whether they like your products or services, point out possible flaws, or make recommendations. If your product got a negative review from the review sites, you may need to address the issue right away by providing appropriate explanation while maintaining a calm tone.

You may also need to publish content that can quash the negative review. You may need to publish fresh, high quality content regularly and try to bury the negative materials that affect your online reputation.

Aside from the reviews of legit customers who bought the product there are also those who were paid to create fake negative reviews. There are also those who simply want to make things difficult for the involved company. You need to be prudent in determining the source of the negative content regarding your brand or company. Deal with the issue in a calm and professional manner.

Chapter 9: Best Examples of Successful ORM

Social media is responsible for giving voice to everyone. Net surfers are no longer just viewers or spectators that lurk the net and be the first to know if there's something new.

There was an online community even before, but it was so quiet that most people thought there was none. The silence was deafening. Now, it's different. The online community is buzzing with new things to talk about.

When people experience something bad with a certain product or company, they quickly tell it to the world via social media. Some even create negative reviews on that particular product.

However, when people are happy with the product or company, they also don't hesitate to share it to the world. A satisfied customer will naturally leave positive review, and that is the one you should aim for – a good impression and image.

Below are a few examples of successful online reputation management.

Samovar Tea Lounge and its 1-Star Review on Yelp

A restaurant customer in San Francisco rated Samovar Tea Lounge with a one star on Yelp and even wrote a long narrative of her experience. She must have listed a number of issues because the owner did not waste time addressing every issue that she had written. The owner took each complaint into consideration. He did not refute the issues that the customer presented. He even assured her that they were doing necessary improvements to meet the satisfaction of the customer.

The owner of Samovar Tea Lounge effectively deflected the unfavorable outcome of a bad review by politely acknowledging the customer's input. He showed his sincerity by directly approaching the customer. He never forgot to show his appreciation to the customer's candor.

It is quite challenging to accept every complaint of the customer, but the owner of the restaurant was able to reply without any trace of anger in his reply. If you are in the same situation, you need to buy some time to gather your thoughts but make sure not to delay it for too long. Making your responses quick and personal can make your client feel cherished.

It is only natural to feel angry when you read something negative about you or your brand, and a one-star review is just too much. In most cases, the initial reaction is to respond in anger. The owner of the remained calm through it all and was able to deliver the right response. He knew that being defensive would only make things worse.

Responding quickly, earnestly, and directly can help you make the complainant view you in a different (positive) light. Luckily, the restaurant owner's quick response (without showing any resentment towards the reviewer) had prevented the negative review from spreading like wildfire.

Starbucks' Free Drink Voucher

Like most service-oriented establishments, Starbucks also experience a service hiccup. Sometimes a drink won't get served on time due to machine malfunction, stock problem, or negligence on the part of a barista. When that happens, the management gives a voucher for a free drink on your next visit. The company makes sure that they offer a first-class customer service policy. They remain consistent with their policy and quick to admit if they made any mistake. They offer simple yet compelling compensation, which gives the customer a feeling of being treated as a VIP.

There are also cases where a customer is the one at fault, but he/she is the customer, and everyone knows that businesses flourish because of customers. A prudent business owner should design a plan on how to provide good customer experience right from the start. There should be a restitution plan, which is suitable for the business, in case some trouble occurs.

The Case of Nike

A business owner who wants to attain success knows he/she needs to have good online reputation to get noticed. The initial reaction is to push out high quality content, associate with thought leaders, and promote news regarding the company. What about the team responsible for monitoring unhappy and unsatisfied customers?

In Nike's case, the company created a support team that has separate Twitter handle. It has the primary task of handling all issues that consumers may have. This simplifies the process that has something to do with consumers. This helps the company to stay focus on other important things that can contribute a lot to the success of the business.

Adespresso says that online platforms provide an amazing avenue for creating and maintaining the company's reputation by giving appropriate response to a blog post or talking to customers on Twitter, Facebook, or other social networking sites. Assigning a dedicated team or spokesperson to methodically handle bad reviews with utmost care can lessen the pressure on other employees. They will become more productive than before when that happens because they don't need to deal with negative reviews or content anymore.

The reputation management team is a significant part of any business plan. Your choice to remain transparent and honest throughout the entire process only proves that you cherish your customers and they will be able to feel your sincerity. Concentrate on customer service, make quick response to bad reviews, and give compensation when necessary.

The reputation management team should take great importance on different communication channels (like blog posts, social media, email, and more), amount of time it takes to solve a certain problem, and the most suitable time to respond.

Whole Foods' Explanation

Whole Foods has natural, great selection of food as well as clothing and household items. Actually, the company has a good reputation. Like most businesses, Whole Foods also have their share of controversy online. What makes this company more amazing is the way they cleaned up their mess.

John Mackey, CEO of Whole Foods, wrote an Op/Ed that many people had read and raised a controversy. John revealed his stance on President Obama's healthcare reform. His opinion created uproar among the company's customers. Some went as far as organizing boycott groups on social media.

They realized the severity of the situation and how it might further affect the company. Whole Foods decided to give a response statement on Facebook after two days. They cleared things up and thanked the people who voiced out their opinion on the matter. Whole Foods preserved their reputation as a company that cares.

JetBlue's Plight

It is annoying to have your flight pushed back, cancelled, or delayed without apparent reason or even a bit of explanation. Some staff members choose to turn a blind eye or don't give sufficient information regarding the cause of cancellation or delay.

It is typical for people in the modern era to vent their frustration on social media. Delayed or cancelled flights are also common that most airline companies just let the passengers rant all they want. Most airline companies do, but not JetBlue.

According to Social Media Examiner, JetBlue is eager to respond and extend some assistance to frustrated clients as soon as possible. An irritated passenger tweeted that he had a delayed flight and was hoping for JetBlue to take him home soon. An hour later, JetBlue tweeted and asked for the passenger's flight number and assured him that they will get an update. The passenger gave his flight number and added that the plane was still in New York. JetBlue informed the passenger about the current schedule of his flight and promised to send him home as soon as possible.

JetBlue understands how important customer loyalty is, and it is also one of the reasons for their popularity. When their passenger complains about cancellation or delay, they immediately communicate with the concerned party and give substantial answer. JetBlue helps the customers solve their predicament.

The given examples are just some of the best examples of successful ORM. Unfortunately, there are more stories about failed online reputation management. You need to know them too so you can prevent yourself from committing the same mistakes.

Chapter 10: Your Ultimate Guide in Creating Good Online Reputation

Before we proceed to some samples of failed ORM, it is best to discuss the complete guide in creating a good online reputation. You already learned some of them in previous chapters and you will learn the rest of them in this chapter. We just add some more points on the things that are previously discussed or mentioned.

There are business owners who will only consider online reputation management when they badly need one. Negative blog posts and reviews can affect a business, especially when the company just keeps ignoring them. These business owners must have thought that the negative materials and rumors about their company or brand will eventually die and everything will return to normal.

The most crucial thing to remember about ORM is that it is one of those things that can give you immense benefits if you implement it right away even though you still have no actual need for it. It is best for you to establish a positive online reputation now if you have not begun yet. You also need to begin fostering positive online properties to offset negative reviews, news, and other materials that may affect your good reputation.

The reputation management activity has 3 main steps. The first one is to create smoke and use as many strong sites and relevant sites with positive conte to take search engine's first top results. The second step is to make sure the the sites represent your client's best image and keep boosting strength on the positive links pushing the negative links down. Finally, the last step does the of work of making the positive sites so strong that even newer negative news can have trouble making top results, we call it "bullet proof" the client. Here are some techniques that help you do it.

Develop Your Own Website

You already know how important it is to have your own website when you want to establish positive reputation online.

There's a huge possibility that you have a website for your business. However, you also need to have a separate website bearing your own name. Let's say your name is Sylvia Smith, you can use SylviaSmith.com as your personal website.

The online community or people who are searching for you can easily locate you if you do that. Websites that bear the exact name of the person or business in their domain typically lands on the first page (top rank) of the search results when someone searches for the specific name. You will get the most number of clicks and continue to occupy the number one spot in the search list and prevent a decent number of people from browsing through the rest of the list.

Buy Related Domains

BrandYourself's CEO and co-founder suggested buying some domain names to help you establish positive online image. For a beginner who is yet to make his/her presence in the online community known, it may be costly and impractical. However, if you are already in a position where you want to take it to the next level, buying other domains for yourself or business is a wise investment.

All hosting companies have negative information about them and the search results always reveal those materials. They have bad reviews and groups that go against them. It just shows how tight the competition is between the hosting companies. As you look at the results, no hosting company seems to be good and reliable. Should the searcher believe the negative things they see, or should they make their own investigation regarding the matter?

We already mentioned that your detractors will do everything to bring you down and may even pay someone to do it on their behalf (cyber criminals or hackers usually accept the job). Someone may choose to write fake negative reviews or comments to mislead potential customers of the involved party. Go Daddy successfully handled this by creating a number of additional websites that have domains with their company name in it.

Comcast did the same thing as Go Daddy, except they prefer to use sub domains. They have their official site named Comcast.com. They used a sub domain for their customer support and named it Customer.Comcast.com. You can do the same if you want.

For example, your main website is SoManyBusiness.com and you can have the following sub domains:

- for your blog: Blog.SoManyBusiness.com or SoManyBusinessblog.com

- for your apps: Apps.SoManyBusiness.com or SoManyBusinessapps.com

- for your products: Product.SoManyBusiness.com

- for customer support: Support.SoManyBusiness.com

Create Multiple Blogs

You can create a number of blogs aside from your company or personal blog. Google Direct Connect and Google+ Authorship can help you inform Google about a blog that have topics associated to you.

Go Daddy's founder Bob Parson has a separate personal blog. He added "Go Daddy Executive Chairman" in the blog's title. Like Bob Parson, you can get creative and rank a few blogs under your name.

You can link the blogs to your Google+ profile with the help of Google Authorship. It is important that your name should appear in the main blog's SEO title.

You can convince your key employees to put up their own blogs (just make sure that they will be able to provide quality materials) with your company name included in their blog.

On the websites you create, it's imperative to make sure the website is well viewed by search engines. Having site maps, enabling search bots, having a structured content with quality and length. There are more than 200 factors for search engine rankings and many sites that can audit your website like verifyseo.com.

Other big factors to consider when making your sites popular and more visible is to get links from other sites (often called backlinks), get shares and likes on social media from your web page and also keep visitors engaged on your site by interacting with it and spending time going through it.

That's when the SEO techniques come in. Having a team that has experience in SEO techniques can come a long way helping your links and your positive content to be more visible in search engine and social media.

Social Media is Your Friend, Get Involved as much as Possible

Having different social media accounts may be a good thing, only if you can maintain and update them regularly. There's no point in creating lots of different social accounts if you don't intend to touch them again. They won't be of any help to your online reputation management. Choose to create a number of strong social profiles on highly popular social media. You need to allot time to keep them up to date and active.

It is also important to build a strong audience on your chosen social networks. You should somehow be able to calculate the number of connections or links to your profile by looking at your audience. The strength in number is undeniable.

The most popular websites that allows users to post content are some of the best social profiles that can help you establish your business and positive online image. You can use Facebook, Twitter, Youtube, Instagram, Tumblr, Blogger, Medium and many others.

Although it may seem laughable to add Myspace in the list, it still ranks pretty well and can bring you many advantages. When using Pinterest, you must include your business name or your name in one of your pins.

You can use pages for business and profiles for people in the following:

1. Wikipedia

2. LinkedIn

3. Facebook

4. Google+

It also helps if you occasionally put your company or personal name in a status update.

It is recommended to use your company or personal name when creating your profile. When you upload a profile photo, the filename should contain your business or personal name. Let's say you are going to upload a photo for your So Many Business profile. You should name the file name of the photo as SoManyBusiness.jpg.

There are thousands of social networks but you don't need all of them. You only need to have 10 to 15 strong networks to work with and you need to update and maintain all of them to render them useful and effective. 10 to 15 social profiles are also enough to fill up the first page of your search engine's search list. You can also visit Knowem if you want to look for niche-specific networks.

Your Online Business Cards

There's no such thing as online business card, but you can create something that resembles it. There are websites that allow you to make your own personalized page that shows your short bio along with your website, social networks, and blog links. About.me is possibly the most favored one. You may also want to try Flavors.me and Dooid.me. To make sure that your business card shows up in the search results, use your personal name or the name of your company.

Claim Your Local Directory Listing

If you have a local business, it is important to claim your local directory listings and profiles. You can create them yourself if they still don't appear on sites like Yahoo Local, Merchant Circle, Yelp, and similar sites. This can also help you connect with local customers who can boost your online reputation. Just make sure to give them the best customer experience so they talk about more positive things regarding your brand. They may even recommend you and your business to other people that they know.

Be a Guest Writer

When you have decided to write guest posts, don't just aim for a one time only guest posting where your name will barely make it in the by-line. The readers will not remember you and if you did a great job, the one who will benefit from it is only the site owner. It could be considered as your good fortune if some readers notice your name and try to check you out.

Aim to write for sites that provide a bio page for the author or let you write your own profile. You have better chances of making your author page pop up in search results if you write for bigger websites. Having links back yo your sites also help search engine rankings. Try to write for websites like Entrepreneur, Forbes, Mashable, TechCrunch, and similar sites.

Agree to do an Interview

If someone asked you for an interview and the interviewee will feature in his/her podcast, video, or blog, don't hesitate and just do it. Most of the time, your name or your business name will be included in the title of the material. It is a good opportunity to get people to know more about you. If it's good, expect it to have a good ranking in the search results.

Spread Your Images Online

One way to spread your image online is through guest posting. You can also place a lot of images online when you create different social profiles with your photo in it. You can also add your photos or images associated to you or your brand on your website (business and personal) and blogs.

Spreading images of yourself all over the net may seem like you're a vain person, but doing so can activate image search results for your brand, company, or name to show. This also pushes down the negative search results that are associated to you or your brand.

If you would like to embed your picture on a website, you can use this format:

<img src="name.jpg" alt="Given Name Surname" title="Given Name Surname" />

Let's say you're name is Leticia Jones and you would like to embed your photo, do it like this:

<img src="Leticia Jones.jpg" alt="Leticia Jones" title="Leticia Jones" />

Doing it like the sample above can give you the best chance of making your image appear in search results and lead searchers to your website.

Create Videos

You can also dominate the results via video. Google owned YouTube and it is wise to post your video in the said site if you want to have better chances of appearing in the search results.

You can also post your video in Vimeo and other similar sites that have the same or almost the same popularity.

Like your photos, you must also include your name or that of your business in the title and description of the video. You will gain some bonus points in SEO if you include your name in the filename of the video.

Issue Press Releases

Your website has a page called media kit that holds all the information bloggers or journalists may need if they want to know more about your company. It also features the latest press releases that you have. A steady stream of fresh press releases can help boost the reputation of your company because it shows that your business is making progress. Bloggers and journalists who have an immediate need for some information about your company may choose to visit your media kit and gather the information that they can obtain immediately. You can also control the content that they are going to publish when that happens.

If you need to make some clarifications regarding a certain issue that negatively affects your reputation, writing a press release is a wise decision. You can email the press release or share it on social networks. Press releases can also help you push down the negative content, which can affect your good online presence, in the search results.

There are press release services, like PRWeb, SBWire, and PR.com, that you can avail when you need it.

Having links from reputable news sites can also help your search engine rankings. These sites are trusted by search engines and getting a link from them, means they trust you too.

It is Important to Interlink

You have numerous opportunities to create a positive reputation and it is necessary to have links to them all. This strategy is called "backlinking" and it's considered today one of the most important aspects of ranking for search engines. When possible, you also need to interlink your good online properties. If there is something that you want to rank, one way to do it is to create backlinks.

The following are some of the things you can do:

- If you something noteworthy, add it to the profile links section of your Google+ and make sure to classify general related links, site links you contribute to, and social profile links.

- Whenever applicable, link your sub domains and blogs to your principal website.

- If you have videos, embed them into your blog content. Go to your social networks and share them.

- You can also add links to your author bio pages (guest postings), Kindle books, apps, podcasts, etc. in the content of your blog.

- See to it that your blog and website link out to your profiles in local search and social networks.

- It is important that each social profile that you have is link out to your blog and website.

You are already aware that you need to monitor your online reputation regularly and not just when you feel like doing it. You must immediately check out the alerts being sent to you to know if there's anything that needs to be dealt with right away. Most of the time, not dealing with it on the spot or completely ignoring the situation that is in urgent need of your attention may lead to more trouble later. Be diligent enough to act on them without delay, it is for your own good.

Respond to your critics in a constructive way and don't let yourself get swayed by your emotions. Your detractors are happier to see you getting emotional and throwing words that could hurt your reputation more than your enemy.

Always think before you open your mouth and the same goes with your staff. Teach everyone in your team to remain calm and vigilant.

Your detractors may seek out the names of your employees and track their activities in their social networks. Whatever they say about your company may affect you and your brand positively or negatively. While defending yourself, you are also trying to prove to your audience that you, your staff, and your entire company are simply awesome.

Search Queries

Many big websites have a search functionality and their page results can be considered a link in the eyes of a search engine. For example: amazon.com/?search=your_business_name can become a actual link in the search results and help push down negative links.

SEO on Page

There are some technical aspects of your website that can improve your search engine rankings. Make sure you have covered them so you win more chances to overcome bad links.

Is your site responsive and fast? These are two important factors that search engines like. You can test your site on Google Page Speed Insights or GTMetrix.

Is you site secure? Adding SSL to your site should help boosting your ranking. SSL is also referred as the 'green lock' or HTTPS. It means all traffic on your site is encrypted and thus more secure.

Make sure your imagens have alt text, title and description. Also, try naming your images with the keywords you want them to appear.

Is your site well structure? By dividing articles into categories and tags, you can help search engines understand the structure of your information. Many Content Management System like Wordpress or Drupal can do that automatically.

Another great tool for Wordpress users is Yoast SEO. Yoast SEO helps you write articles and structure them in such way that boosts your chance of getting better ranking. There are some other options available, but having some experience with Yoast SEO, will definitely make you a better writer for the internet.

Content is King

The gold rule of SEO is: Content is King. That means that content that are relevant and brings value to readers will eventually have better ranking scores.

Put effort in writing compelling articles that people will be happy to land their eyes on. Writing guides, tutorials, how-tos are excellent choices.

You can use some viral strategies, and even add a link bait title, **but do not fall into fake news.** If you have some amazing news to spread, check your sources first.

An appealing title can help you get clicks on search engines and social media. You can play with link baits titles but never play with your reader's trust.

Once the users land on your page, it's important to keep them spending time and interacting in your page. If they click on you page and then press back, it shows the search engines that your result it not what they want.

By having an appealing content and related articles you can help keep the user in your site increasing time on site and reducing bounce rate.

There are some techniques like adding a popup or having the user click to display the rest of the article. Such techniques may be considered bad practices for search engines, so make you sure you do your research first.

Ask you team to starting sharing, liking and commenting the news you are releasing to create momentum and social proof.

Backlinks Software

Although it's not best practices, many SEO firms and SEO professionals use software to manipulate Search Engines results. These softwares create fake accounts and create automated content that links to your main sites thus increasing their authority. There are also sites that simulates search engines searches and clicks to increase Click-through rate and time on site. Other softwares have thousand of robot accounts to like, share and comment on social media creating more popularity for your websites.

Although these software might work, be aware that the search engines algorithms are evolving and trying to detect those tricks. Plus, without a great compelling content, your effort may be in vain.

Managing Crisis

Clients will come most often when there is a crisis. Being a professional online reputation manager means knows how to handle situations like these.

The most important thing is to keep positive and calm.

Make sure everybody who are involved understand the situation and have empathy on the subject.

Do not attack back. Leave the lawyers to do the *fighting* and remove anyone on the team that may lose their temper.

If a mistake is made, no matter the size, write an sincere apology note and try to fix the problem. Make sure your reply is thoughtful, transparent and ethical.

Go back to the company's or person's core values and passion. Our goal is to create a better world and by creating a better world, by helping others, we create value that becomes a product or service. Make sure your client's core values and passions are well remembered and apologize for any mistakes as well state all the corrections that are into action.

If the situation presented is unfair to the company or person's, let the followers defend them.

Use social media and sites to state your reply. Work on the plan to fix your processes so it won't happen again.

Once the bad viral momentum is about to be over, stretch the momentum with a recovery plan that is viral, positive and ethical.

Keep working on the recovery momentum to gain back people's trust. Learn the lesson and improve.

Chapter 11: Sample Cases of Failed ORM

This chapter presents the failed online reputation management, and hopefully you will refrain yourself from following the same path. The sample cases aim to give you a clear scenario about what might happen to your brand and you if you do the things they did.

Aside from unsatisfied customers, you also need to deal with your detractors and competitors that may use underhanded means to agitate you and make you do things that could ruin your reputation. Often, the situation is not the one that makes you feel happy or angry but your reaction to it. A certain situation may seem to put you in a compromising position, but when you try to remain calm and not get emotional about it you will see that it is not as grave as you think.

Take these cases as opening samples of failed online reputation management:

1. Dark Horse Café

Dark Horse Café received a tweet from one of their customers complaining about their lack of electrical outlets when most of their clients are office workers who carry their own laptop. Dark Horse Café is quick to give their response, which shows they are into their customers. However, their response to that particular customer's tweet was they are in coffee business and not the office business and they have many outlets that allow them to do what they need to do.

The response effectively displayed their insolence towards their customer who merely pointed out that it would be better if they have more electrical outlets for their loyal customers who may need to use their laptops to take care of an urgent matter. Their aggressive behavior became famous in the online community and caused severe damage on the company's online reputation.

The famous case happened in 2010 and people still talk about it even now. The undying discussion about it constantly reminds people that the company is only interested in running their business and does not care about their customers. The case continues to give Dark Horse Café negative online reputation. If you want to survive in the competitive business world, you need to be mindful of the things you say and do. One false move can lead to your end.

It was just a simple complain from the customer and a simple explanation or promise could've been enough to appease the customer. Instead of pacifying the customer, the café chose to ignite the ire of the online community.

2. Amy's Baking Company

This company chose to fight fire with fire when they received a one-star review on the net. They barraged the reviewer with insults. The local news picked up the gist of it and spread it. Amy's Baking Company got a negative publicity that affected their business.

They should've just accepted the rating and showed their sincerity by doing everything they can to improve their services and/or products.

Do not fool yourself into thinking that people are not discussing things about you. The best way to quash demeaning criticisms that may greatly affect your reputation is to deal with them immediately but in a calm manner. Sometimes, all it takes (to bring back peace or preserve it) is proper explanation.

Epic Fails and Lessons Learned

There are countless examples of failed ORM and some of them may dismay or just amuse you. This chapter aims to teach you some lessons and not copy the companies that failed miserably in their online reputation management at some point in their entire business operation.

Get to know some of them, understand where they fail, and learn the lessons from such mistakes. The successful ORMs that were presented earlier should've given you inspiration and ideas on how to handle certain situations with decisiveness without losing your patience and self-respect. The epic ORM fails are here to remind you about the things that you need to refrain from doing.

1. American Airlines

At first glance, there seems to be nothing wrong in sending an automated tweet to a customer but it makes it less personal. Businesses that render services should always take time to personally respond to a customer's query. But, American Airlines tweeted a disgruntled customer on February of 2013 thanking him for his support instead of offering an apology. Such action from the company only added insult to injury. It was even more painful to learn that the company did not make an effort to reply with sincerity because it used an automated tweet when they should've personally consoled the passenger.

American Airlines' online reputation management failed because:

- They sent automated response tweet without even looking or checking the customer's complaint. Sending an automated tweet is bad enough and sending the wrong response makes it worse. Human edited tweets and replies are way better and more precise than machine-generated responses.

While it is a wise move to respond to customers, especially when they are angry, machine-generated response is not an option. In the said case, the company just made a fool of themselves for all online community to see and even managed to anger the customer even more.

If you are in a business of providing services to customers, it is best not to automate anything online. You surely wouldn't dare automate your client's service experience when facing him/her in person, you also shouldn't do it online.

2. National Rifle Association (NRA)

The American Rifleman, which is the Twitter account associated with NRA, tweeted a simple greeting to shooters and asking about their weekend plans (the tweet happened in Friday of July, 2012). The tweet was innocent but the timing was wrong. It was posted on the same day that Aurora, Colorado experienced a tragic shooting incident in one of its theatre. It was truly unfortunate for Colorado and NRA. The tweet could be pre-scheduled and just happened to coincide with the tragic shooting, but Twitter users found it inappropriate considering the shooting episode that also happened that same day. It was early morning when the tweet was posted, and it was removed shortly at noon. American Rifleman's Twitter account was entirely deleted later in the day. Media outlets contended that the PR contact of NRA claimed to be unaware of the existence of the unfortunate tweet.

NRA failed to effectively manage their online reputation because:

- Their posted tweet was not appropriate given the current social climate and event at the time.

- They did not re-check the pre-scheduled tweet before posting it and make sure that it remained appropriate.

- Instead of posting an apology and accepting responsibility to the said event, they chose to deny the existence of the tweet.

- They did react immediately.

ORM experts may disagree over the decision to keep the tweet posted and hold the company involved accountable or delete the post. The first lesson in the given case is to keep yourself aware and stay attuned to the current events. The next lesson is to check the outgoing posts at least two or three times and make sure that they are appropriate. If there's a certain controversy or event that has potential affiliation with your company or brand, you must be prudent and careful when posting or sharing something in your social networks.

The account, American Rifleman, could have chosen to be honest from the beginning. They should have admitted that they did not know about the shooting incident in Colorado when they posted a pre-prescheduled tweet. Moreover, they should have sent their sentiments to all of the shooting incident victims at the time as well as their families. Their failure to apologize and accept responsibility for the offense only made things worse.

It is easy to delete an account, but it cannot be considered as a sort of damage control. The damage has been done and screenshots of it will naturally get posted for other people to know.

3. JPMorgan

Jimmy Lee, JPMorgan's top executive, was assigned to handle the company's Twitter Q&A. The Q&A with the #AskJPMorgan was opened in November, 2013. JPMorgan was bombarded with series of unfavorable events that affected its reputation and the purpose of Twitter Q&A was to improve the company's public relations.

They started slow but the company did not anticipate that they would be asked about their latest legal issue. They also need to answer the different inquiries regarding their supposed to be responsible social practices. They also received a lot of insults from different people.

There were a lot of responses from different groups of people. In the entire tweets that they received, more than 66% were negative reactions. JPMorgan Chase decided to cancel their Twitter Q&A and openly admitted that it was a terrible scheme.

JPMorgan failed because:

- They were overconfident and had inadequate knowledge (or lack of understanding) of how people perceive their brand or company.

- They were not able to establish good guesses regarding the possible results of their plan.

- Their post lacked aptness considering their current situation, popular opinion about them, and people's sentiments.

To avoid such failure, you must check things thoroughly first before you do something that can harm your reputation even more. The plan to have a Q&A is actually a good thing and it proves the company's willingness to practice transparency and openness. However, in JPMorgan's case the time was wrong. Instead of suppressing the public's anger, JPMorgan provided an opportunity for people to openly vent their frustrations. If you want to do the same thing, know the public sentiment regarding your company first and have a backup plan in case it begins to go out of hand. JPMorgan wanted to get close to the people but did not consider the public sentiment at the time.

Also, JPMorgan Chase learned that it was easy to control the frequency or amount of incoming questions if you will do it in person and not online. The JPMorgan's Twitter Q&A received thousands of questions all at once. They failed to control the incoming questions and received a fatal blow in the end. It also proved that knowing the current situations and public sentiments before deciding to go online can help you avoid possible humiliation and damage to your reputation. In such situation, employing traditional PR first along with strategic ORM practices would've given better results.

4. Kitchen Aid

The Twitter account of Kitchen Aid USA suffered a hard blow when they posted an impolite tweet regarding the deceased grandmother of President Obama in October, 2012. The post landed on the company's Twitter account instead of the company staff's account who wrote it. Although the unpleasant tweet was immediately removed, they were not quick enough because screenshots of the tweet had already been taken. The head of Kitchen Aid Brand, Cynthia Soledad, made several tweets of personal apology to President Obama and his family as well as everyone on Twitter. In her tweet, the head of Kitchen Aid Brand stated her name and position and then the apology and explanation.

Kitchen Aid managed to quickly address the offense made by their staff. There were users who lashed back that they would cease to patronize Kitchen Aid as their preferred appliance provider. Kitchen Aid properly gave an explanation about the careless mistake of their staff and promised everyone that the said staff will no longer tweet for them.

Kitchen Aid's online reputation management failed because:

- The staff who posted the tweet did not properly check the account that he/she was using at the time. Regardless of what you want to share or tweet, make certain that you are using the right account.

- The one who made the post did not bother checking after he/she made the post. The post could have been deleted right away (before screenshots were made) as soon as it has been verified that wrong account was used.

It is prudent to always double check your tweet or post before and after you made them. Kitchen Aid successfully mitigated the situation due to their quick response. Nonetheless, the event that happened can still be considered ORM failure on Kitchen Aid's part. They set a fine example of what a company should do during such time and that is to immediately apologize and take responsibility along with a proper explanation.

Cynthia Soledad could've chosen not to introduce herself but she might have felt that she needed to, and in turn it added human element to the account. Since humans are prone to making mistakes, the addition of human element somehow made it easier for everyone to forgive the incident. Cynthia Soledad's action proved that it is still possible to salvage brand image despite the occurrence of such incident. Taking immediate steps to address a problem can help soften the blow to the company's online reputation and keep the damage nominal.

5. Nestlé

A few years ago, Nestlé was criticized regarding their environmental practices and received negative comments from the public. The company chose to ignore the comments and did not address them properly. People became furious and posted the company's logo in altered version. The name "Kit Kat" in the logo was altered into "Killer" and the rest of the design remained the same.

It was during the early part of 2010 that Greenpeace began a campaign against Nestlé via a web video. The non-governmental environmental organization called Greenpeace encouraged their supporters to change their profile pictures to something that clearly indicate their displeasure to Nestlé. Users wrote their sentiments on the Facebook fan page of Nestlé using the altered version of the company's logo.

Nestlé ignored the messages but took time to ask the people with the altered logo as profile picture to stop using any version of the company's logo. They would take such action of the users as copyright infringement and would delete the posted comments. The announcement that the page administrator made only added more oil to the fire as more people got angrier. The representative of Nestlé apologized for giving such comments that made the online mob angrier. The company has decided that it was best to close their public page.

Nestlé's online reputation management failed because:

- They tried to deal with their social media catastrophe even though they lack appropriate plan of action.

- Instead of pacifying the people's anger, the company even told them about the things they need to do and not to do.

- They panicked and tried to manipulate the furious mob.

People will be forced to take actions if the company continues to ignore the important issues or find solution to a particular problem. It is foolish to argue with consumers, regardless if you're right or wrong. It is not a good idea to argue with people about their sentiments and instruct them to do things when they already want to beat you up. When the public is already angry, it is best to apologize and don't hesitate to take responsibility and action before they get angrier. Show your utmost sincerity and assure the customers that you heard them.

6. Microsoft

Microsoft introduced Tay the Twitter bot on March 23, 2016. Microsoft described that it was an experiment and it was designed to comprehend conversation. Apparently, the experimental bot should get smarter as it communicates with different people. Regrettably, it did not take 24 hours for things to escalate immediately. Tay was pretty innocent in the beginning and got corrupted soon after. Tay managed to push out many tweets that may make you wince.

Tay is like a child that cannot decipher good from bad and needs an adult to guide her and be a fine lady someday. However, if the one guiding her is not teaching her anything good, she will definitely go astray.

Probably, most of the inputs she received from the ones she communicated with could only be described as appalling and horrendous. Tay managed to gather the bits and pieces of those atrocious inputs, collated them, and randomly posted them in her tweets.

The next day, Microsoft began deleting some of the offensive tweets that Tay posted. The company apologized and cancelled their project.

Microsoft's online reputation management failed because:

- The company did not think that automated tweets could harm them or was over confident that the project would surely succeed. At this point, the technology that can produce flawless response is yet to be discovered and it is safer to have human edited responses.

- They did not monitor carefully despite the fact that they just launched their project. They could have prevented it from becoming too big if they were able to delete the bad tweets to avoid offending others.

If you have a project on its experimental stage (like Microsoft and their tweets), it is best to have a backup plan available and countermeasure must be prepared. It is also important to think about all the unfavorable things that may occur in order to avoid it or at least soften the blow.

It was a good thing that Microsoft was able to react fairly quickly and apologized. Their actions helped pacify the public's annoyance and prevented possible irreparable damage on their online reputation.

7. Kenneth Cole

Cairo, Egypt experienced left and right protests in 2011. However, Kenneth Cole just disregarded the seriousness of the events that were happening in Cairo at the time and posted something callous. They used the hashtag#Cairo without even bothering to know its meaning. They used the hashtag to promote their spring collection in Cairo.

The practice of hashtag jacking can be seen as something distasteful and impolite. This is especially true when a company use the hashtag of a momentous event that caught the attention of people around the world in order to promote their merchandise, business, or brand. The company posted a semi apology tweet and explained that they were not trying to overlook the seriousness of the situation in Cairo at the time.

Later, the tweet was removed and Kenneth Cole posted on his Facebook an official apology.

Kenneth Cole's online reputation management failed because:

- They issued a semi apology first and seemed to avoid taking full responsibility for their action.

- The company assumed that the public would accept the idea of making light of a grave incident.

- No matter what they say, hashtag jacking is a serious offense and some callous organizations will take advantage of it to make some profit.

Unlike in previous cases (mentioned in this chapter) of hashtag jacking, Kenneth Cole knew the context of the hashtag. Humor is not that easy for comedians to master, and always keep in mind that each individual may have a different take on what seems to be a humorous situation or coincidence. It is recommended to weigh things carefully before posting or tweeting something that you try to make humorous. It is a good thing the Kenneth Cole did apologize later, although it could've been better if the company did not deliver the semi apology first.

8. Bud Light

Hashtag jacking can create serious trouble for you. Do you know what's worse than hashtag jacking? Creating a hashtag that can make your imagination run wild or with connotations that remind you of the images from traumatic events. Bud Light was under fire in 2015 when they created the hashtag#Upforwhatever just underneath their slogan, which gave an ambiguous meaning. The company was accused of encouraging date rape and it angered the online community.

Alexander Lambercht, Bud Light's vice president, announced that they decided not to use the said hashtag and slogan in their campaign. The company apologized and said they regretted it. What made it worse was that they already used the same hashtag that created trouble for them before (during St. Patrick's Day).

Bud Light's online reputation management failed because:

- The hashtag, which was a mistake, was printed on all of the company's products and people will only remember the event whenever they see it.

- They used the same hashtag again when it already created trouble for them the first time they used it.

- They created a hashtag without comprehending the possible meaning (or it may have double meaning) and how people may perceive it.

When you tweet or post something that didn't work the first time, don't ever think that it will work the next time you use it. Take it as a sort of omen and refrain from using it again even if it seems to be suitable for your next campaign. The company should've tested the hashtag first and see how their customers perceive it before printing it on their products.

It was a good thing that they were able to post an apology on their website and took responsibility. They did not waste time to pacify the public's uproar.

9. ESPN

Gerry Hamilton, ESPN's recruiting analyst tried to post a tweet with video about a football recruit. Unfortunately, he inadvertently posted a pornographic video link to his more than 15,000 followers. He was able to delete the tweet within minutes, but screenshots of it had already been taken and spread on the internet. Later, another tweet was posted with the correct video link.

The analyst did not comment on his error. The adult video site reached out to the analyst and made it worst when the people behind it had decided to poke fun at him for his failure to manage his online reputation. The fuming mob tweeted their anger on the lack of online reputation management action on the part of the analyst and ESPN. The media outlets reported that the offender did not make any public apology and ESPN was unavailable to make their statement. The public felt that ESPN and Hamilton planned to brush it off as if nothing of the sort happened. There was no proof that Hamilton paid a penalty for his mistake. On the contrary, Hamilton even won more followers after going through such ordeal. Today, he has more than 26,000 followers under his name.

ESPN's online reputation management failed because:

- The one who posted the tweet did not double check the link that he inserted.

- Hamilton did not check his materials prior to his post and only decided to check it minutes after he tweeted.

If the situation escalated into something more difficult to handle, not taking accountability and not apologizing for the offense made could also be blamed for his failure to manage his online reputation and dragged the company along with him. However, he did gain more followers after the unfortunate incident. He was also able to delete the post immediately, but still not quick enough as screenshots were taken. At least, not many people had actually seen the actual tweet (not just the screenshot).

Deleting the offensive tweet right after posting it was probably the best solution and the simplest. But, if it took him some time to delete it and many people had seen it, brushing it off like that wouldn't be enough. Since Hamilton was not admonished for the incident that happened, it was apparently considered as a forgiven mistake. However, the actions of the company and the analyst of sweeping the dirt under the rug left a bitter taste.

Another company that showed a classic example of hashtag jacking fail was DiGiorno Pizza. They used #WhyIStayed to promote their pizza, but the hashtag was originally used to give emphasis on domestic violence and why there are people who decided to stay. The tweet was deleted quickly and

DiGiorno apologized immediately. They admitted that they did not read about the context of the said hashtag before they used it in their post. The company did not lose (much) face on the said incident. Their online reputation management can be considered superb at the time. They even wrote a personalized apology to everyone who commented.

Keep the lessons you've learned in these cases in mind and prevent yourself from committing them. The next chapter will further discuss the lessons you've learned here and then some. Treasure the good and throw away the bad.

Chapter 12: Reputation Management Mistakes to Avoid

In the last chapter, you have seen some of the companies with failed ORM. Some of them got back on their feet pretty quickly and some are still trying to recover from their losses. Don't expect that today's people will just stay quiet and do nothing when they see something's not quite right, especially when they have lots of ways to voice out their opinions or views.

In this chapter, you will learn the mistakes that you need to avoid in managing your online reputation. Aside from the lessons you've learned from the previous chapter, we will discuss other mistakes that were not tackled before. Learning from your mistakes can make you stronger and more mature, learning from others' mistakes and preventing yourself from following the same path is way even better.

We all know the importance of social media in creating and maintaining a person's online reputation or that of a certain company, brand, and organization. Small business owners usually rely on social media to connect with their customers and share anecdotes that can help them shine. However, misuse of social media could lead to great disaster.

Below, you will find the reputation management mistakes that you need to avoid.

Mistake #1: Choosing a Person Who's Not Capable of Handling the Social Media Accounts

Most companies have accounts on different social networks and it is advisable to do so if you want to reach out to your customers. There are customers who own an account or two (probably more) on each of the most popular social networks, and there are also those who own only one account on a particular social media outfit.

Managing the different accounts on your own plus doing some other things for your business will surely drain your energy. Instead of helping your business flourish, you may only neglect the most important things in running your business because you are too busy managing your different social media accounts. You can assign one of your staff or hire someone to take care of that for you, so you can focus on the things that need your attention.

However, choosing the wrong person to handle such task can bring more harm than good. When you go back to some of the cases in the previous chapter, the usual culprit in sending inappropriate or wrong tweets were the staff

When you assign someone to manage the different accounts, make sure that your chosen person is capable enough to handle them. Most companies just randomly choose a person to manage the social media accounts without even testing the capability of that person. You need to ask these following questions:

- Does the chosen person know how to deal with all types of people?

- Is the chosen person tactful?

- Does he/she know how to handle the different social media accounts of your company?

- Is he/she diligent enough?

You can add more to the list if you have other questions in mind. Your social media posts reflect who you are. Whatever you or the assigned staff posted on that social media account may affect your online reputation, either positive or negative. That's why it is important to assign someone who can make the company proud and not cause its demise (just look back at the cases of the failed ORM). You communicate with your customers regularly via the social media, and it is important that the person handling all the social media accounts of the company is someone you can depend on. That person should be able to safeguard your good online reputation and help boost it.

Mistake #2: Being Emotional and Personal

There are times when everything seems to go wrong, and you let your emotions get the best of you. If you own a business, you should always keep an open mind and refrain from expressing your innermost thoughts regarding the current events when you post something on the social media profiles of your company.

Avoid discussing something about politics, religion, and other controversial topics that may offend some people that matter to you. However, if the controversial topic is related to your business, just try to be careful with your words to avoid unfavorable situations.

It is important that you remain unbiased or keep your tone neutral. If you want to appeal to everyone (or most people), it is prudent to avoid conflict-ridden topics that may put you in a position where you must make a choice. The online accounts that you use for your business must not contain your personal views.

You and your customers as well as employees may share the same principles and moral values, but there are still certain areas that both parties may not agree. Be careful not to post anything that could sow discord between you and the people that are loyal to your business or your potential customers. Try to keep your true sentiments hidden, especially if you strongly favor a particular cause that most people in your industry do not.

Before you post something, try to determine first if it's something that can be considered controversial that may affect your business no matter what you say. For example, if you are selling arts and crafts materials, it's improbable that your customers would be displeased regarding a post endorsing a particular brand of thread or hook. However, they may not be happy to see a particular political candidate's endorsement in your post.

Mistake #3: Ignoring or Removing Negative Comments

Negative comments are usually painful to read, but they can help you improve your business a lot. People post negative comments when they see or feel that something is amiss or did not meet their expectations. Don't take hurtful words to heart and just treat them as reminders that you need to do something about the areas or things that they complain about regarding your business or brand. You need to read the negative comments, so you will know what to do.

Sometimes it's difficult to finish reading the entire negative comment of a customer due to the upsetting or unkind words. But, it is advisable to finish reading the entire comment because some even give suggestions or things that you can improve on to make your business flourish. Customers who want to see you improve will naturally support you and give some inputs regarding the things that you can do for your business and make everyone happy.

Ignoring or deleting negative comments posted by the customers may lead to misunderstanding, especially when a customer left some suggestions for you to review. When you delete the negative comments, customers may think that you don't seriously take their issues and treat them as nothing important. If the customer posted some suggestions for improvement along with the negative comment and you did not post any response or act according to the suggestion, that person will know that you have decided to ignore his/her post.

Your customers may choose to post complaints about you on all kinds of platforms like forums, social media, blogs, and others. It would be impossible to control the rants once they spread. One way to prevent negative comments from creating too much damage to your online reputation is for you to acknowledge them along with proper action or response.

There are negative comments that do not need any response, but you need to be careful in determining them. Your detractors may also post negative comments on your website and there are times when keeping quiet could be the best solution to your predicament. However, you need to be prudent and smart when determining whether a certain post was made to provoke you or do something to enhance the quality of your brand or services. A timely reply and action can immediately put the negative comments under control.

60% of consumers are looking forward to the company's response to comments and reviews on social media. Looking at the given figure, that's more than half of consumers. Don't be surprised when your online reputation suddenly plummeted just because you failed to associate with your online audience.

It is easy to lose the trust and approval of your customers and not responding to the negative comments or reviews is one of them.

A simple recognition of your mistake and asking an apology for something that's offensive in the eyes of your customers can help you build credibility and trust.

Your customers will keep patronizing your brand when they see your sincerity and desire to give them the best product and services they deserve.

You also need to take time to express your gratitude to your customers that give positive feedback and words of encouragement, which can inspire the whole company to get going and keep striving to be the best. If a customer tweeted that you provide great service, you can re-tweet it and thank the one who posted it. Such action can also help you spread the good word of your customer about you and establish your brand.

Mistake #4: Creating Fake Reviews of Competitors

There are business owners who post negative reviews on the website of their competitors in an attempt to make their opponents less credible. It is an underhanded strategy that is ethically incorrect and absurd. The reviews can also be deleted if they were proven to be inappropriate. Similarly, paying someone to post good reviews on your business website is also unethical.

For instance, inappropriate reviews on Google My Business can be removed as long as the involved party flags them as off-topic, spam, or inappropriate. Conflict of interest, such as misrepresented identity connection with a certain business and paid reviews, can be used as ground for removal of negative reviews. Other business owners do such things, but don't put yourself in the same level as those iniquitous people. Instead of resorting to such despicable act, focus your energy in establishing a positive online reputation.

If you think that your page has fake negative reviews, you can flag them as inappropriate or false and you can click this link if you want to know how to remove the fake reviews.

Mistake #5: Buying Positive Customer Reviews

Paying someone or a group to post positive reviews on your website is not a good practice. In fact, you are cheating if you do that and it has the same bearing as paying someone to create negative reviews for your competitors. Paid endorsements for services or products without disclosure are forbidden under the FTC Endorsement Guidelines.

If a reviewer is closely connected with the company being reviewed, the person writing the review must disclose it in the post. The same goes with the situation wherein the company has compensated the reviewer to write the review. The disclosure can preserve the authenticity of the review. Without proper disclosure, the public's perception regarding the legitimacy of the review gets affected.

The compensation that the review may receive can be anything, including discount coupons, special privilege cards, freebies, and cash. You can generate authentic positive reviews by asking loyal or satisfied customers to leave a review on your website. If you strive to give quality products and services to your customers, you don't need to worry about accumulating too many positive reviews. It is almost impossible not to get negative reviews (aside from the ones that your competitors may try to give) because not everyone has the same preferences.

Also, your authentic positive reviews will give you more benefits and advantages. Negative reviews may come, but they won't be enough to ruin your good reputation.

If you are someone who is just about to start your business, make sure to start creating a good online reputation immediately and manage it without fail. Don't imitate others who only take their online reputation management seriously when trouble come knocking on their door.

Mistake #6: Not Giving any Serious Consideration to Online Reputation Management

Most business owners who want to immediately start profiting may not even give online reputation management some serious consideration. Most of these business owners thought that they don't have online reputation and just decide to begin operating their business. They did not bother to create their online reputation, direct it to help them reach their goal, or even take time to monitor it.

There are business managers or CEOs that refuse to go online or log in to their social media account because they fear that the online community might say negative things about them. It's the same as saying they won't get hurt if they no nothing. On the contrary, keeping themselves in the dark and not doing anything when there's a huge issue that they need to clear, or handle can only ruin the reputation of the company. Their own reputation gets affected as well since they are connected with the company being bombarded with negative comments.

Good or bad, the public will keep discussing the brand or the company along with the people that are connected to it. You need to give your customers an opportunity to talk to you when they encounter some problems with the product, need to inquire something, or would like to complain. By being online all the time, people may feel that you are always there for them and willing to listen no matter what.

You might even have a Yelp profile with caustic reviews and not even aware of its existence. Know that the customers can post reviews about you even if you don't create your own profile on the review sites. It is recommended to have your own profile on the review sites, so you can be recognized as the legit owner and give your reactions or comments. If you don't claim it, there's no way for you to address reviews regarding your company or brand.

Mistake #7: Updating at Irregular Intervals

It is important to update your social media accounts regularly if you want to leave good impression on your followers. Your fans follow your page because they want to know the latest things about you. They expect you to post interesting content at regular basis. Updating at irregular intervals or being inconsistent may drive your fans to un-follow you. Worst, they might even spread their dissatisfaction with you and influence others to do the same.

Posting ten interesting facts in one day and not posting anything in the next couple of weeks may annoy your followers. You are also giving a bad example. If you really need to take care of urgent matters first and don't have time to make updates, don't simply disappear for a long time without giving a heads up. Your fan will understand of you only give them proper explanation and notice so they won't expect too much from you during the time when you cannot update your social media accounts.

If you are having hard time keeping up or you can no longer monitor your accounts properly, you may choose to hire or assign someone capable and trustworthy to handle your social media accounts or try to manage your time efficiently. You may need to cut off some activities that prevent you from being productive or performing your duties well.

You also need to monitor your accounts in case there are issues that must be address immediately and efficiently. Your quick response can help you prevent a problem from escalating into something more troublesome.

Mistake #8: Fighting Fire with Fire

You already know that some business owners pay reviewers to give negative reviews to competitors and it is also possible that you are a victim of fake negative reviews. Should you get angry? It is natural to get mad for something underhanded, especially when your reputation is at stake. However, fighting fire with fire could burn you.

Besides, you don't know for sure (unless you have already investigated) if the negative reviews were done by paid reviewers or legit customers. Even if the negative reviews were indeed fabricated, you must still remain calm and tackle it with presence of mind and without losing your cool.

You can start your response with a simple introduction about yourself just to give them some idea, but don't make it sound like you are trying so hard to sell yourself or your brand. After making your introduction the time is just about right to acknowledge the negative review or complaint and give your sincere apology for the unpleasant experience that the customer endured.

You should not stop with your apology, which did not help you re-instate your good reputation in the eyes of the offended customer. But, it did stop the customer from thinking more negative things about you. You can bring back the customer's trust by presenting the steps that you intend to take in correcting the problem. If you feel that offering a discount is necessary to persuade the customer to give your business another chance, then do so.

It is best to offer discount on their purchase to make them visit your company to avail it. You can also offer a freebie, but you need to make that customer try one of your best-selling items and completely mend the damage to your reputation. Make sure that the customer will be truly satisfied with the next product that he/she is going to buy form you.

Mistake #9: Not Answering Complaints

Although you should not fight fire with fire, it is also wrong to let the serious complaints left unanswered. Some customers can be so unreasonable sometimes and just want to bring trouble to you in exchange of something (like freebies, discounts, special privileges, etc.) or they have nothing better to do.

A good business owner should take time to offer proper explanation and calmly state their side for the public to know. If the customer continues to viciously attack your business, you must calmly respond once more but it would be for the last time. Continuing to respond or fighting the customer head on will only make you look bad. Keep your composure as you prepare to walk away even though nothing was resolved. Try your best to gain more positive reviews to make the negative review appear insignificant.

Keep in mind that it is impossible to please all people, and bad reviews are expected to occur. But, it doesn't mean that it's the end of the line for you and your business when you start getting bad reviews. It is important to analyze whether the review is fabricated or posted by the legit customer. Take note of the things that made the customer unhappy with this/her purchase and take necessary steps to meet the customer's satisfaction. The negative reviews or comments from the customers can serve as your guide as you try to improve your brand.

Mistake #10: Not Giving Good Reviews Enough Attention

You need to respond to negative comments and reviews in a calm manner, and you also need to respond to good reviews.

Most of the time, business owners casually ignore the good reviews since they won't damage the reputation of the company. On the contrary, not giving any response to good reviews may somehow upset the one who gave the review. Customers will naturally expect some sort of response from you and a simple word of thanks for the positive review and patronage is enough to make the customers pledge their undying loyalty to your brand and company.

Responding to positive reviews can help deepen your relationship with your customers. Take note of the things that customers appreciate the most about your product or brand and make sure to continue giving them satisfaction.

Reputation management is not limited only to damage control as some people think. Most business owners pour their energy in answering only negative comments or reviews. Bear in mind that people expect to see your response regardless if it's a negative or positive review.

You need to win the hearts of those who gave you negative reviews, and you also need to maintain the loyalty of the ones who gave you positive reviews. You need to be balanced and give each review a fitting response.

Mistake #11: Not Posting Quality Content

If you don't post quality content, your negative review will only continue to occupy one of the best spots in the search results when people try to find out more about you. Fill the net with content that puts you and your company in a favorable light. Quality content doesn't just mean well written, it needs to add value to your customer showing that your business is in fact making their lives easier and better.

Don't try rehashing your content by writing it in different way because your readers will definitely spot that you have used the material before and just gave it a fresh look. Creating something fresh and giving the old content some fresh look won't cut it.

You can even try press releases, which was suggested in the earlier chapter, when you want people to know something new about you and your company. Post pictures, achievements, new products, newly formed organization, and others that can make your customers or readers to want to know more about you.

Chapter 13: FAQs Regarding Ways to Eliminate Negative Search Results

Anyone can have negative search results, and they can be frustrating and unfair. Negative search results can dramatically affect your chances of enticing investors, attracting customers, or getting hired.

Like you, most people would like to know how to get rid of the negative search results. Understand that you may be able to eliminate the negative search results, but you still need to work hard to create a good online reputation for yourself.

Below are the most frequently asked questions that people have about the ways to eliminate negative search results. Take note that some of the frequently asked questions have already been answered in the previous chapters and no longer included in this list.

1. How can you take down a negative search result?

In Chapter 12, you learned about how to remove negative reviews on Google My Business. Taking down a negative search result can be quite challenging. You need to contact the website owner and make a request to take down the content from his/her website that gives you a negative search result.

You can go to whois.net to know the owner of website that gives your negative search result. You can send an email to the owner and politely ask him/her to delete the damaging material from his/her website. Explain your side and try to get the website owner's sympathy. You can also try to show that you have fixed the things that the negative material had pointed out. Remain polite while saying your piece.

2. Is it better to change the business name instead of waiting for the unfavorable search results to change?

You can choose to change your business name and make a fresh start. But before you do, make sure not to repeat the things that you did the first time. It is important to build your online reputation right away and manage it without fail from day one.

Understand that changing your name might bring confusion to your loyal customers and may not even try the products you offer under your new business name. Also, people who want to find out more about you will definitely do their due diligence and may find the former name of your business.

If you can utterly cut your connections from the business, it may just give you a better chance to have a fresh start. However, you need to weigh the risks first before deciding to follow that route.

3. Is it okay to take legal action right away?

It is quite challenging to get the unwanted search results be removed legally. People are free to say just about anything they want to talk about online. Let's not talk about how strong the case is, the legal process alone can cost you a lot of money and may take years to resolve. If you follow the suggestions in the previous chapters regarding burying negative search results, your unwanted search results may have been buried already before the case has concluded.

If you are still interested to file a case, speak with an attorney. Take note that the lawyer may not give you something that you want to hear and still charge you for his work.

4. Are there any shortcuts?

There are, but internet is evolving in order to kill those shortcuts. Online reputation companies can use SEO techniques to push up your positive content on search engines faster by using connections or software to create backlinks, social media buzz and viral quality content. These firms also use Press Releases and a strict social media management for crisis. You need some amount of patience and diligence to bury negative search results even with the help of SEO techniques. You also need to remain calm because as you try to bury the negative search result, there are people (e.g. your haters and competitors) who will try to prevent you by making sure that you have more negative materials under your name. You need to work hard enough to beat your enemies and restructure your values and processes.

5. Is it possible for negative result that had been pushed down in the search results jump back up?

Google makes regular updates, including search results. The updates on search results are based on relevancy factors. Search result fluctuations are normal. Also, people in different parts of the world may not see the same search results that you see. There are three things that greatly affect the difference in search results:

- Experiments in Algorithm

Google engineers also conduct some experiments in algorithm to enhance user experience. They usually test it on a small group of random users. After searching incognito or deleting your cookies, do you get different search results? If you do, it is possible that the team of engineers may be trying a new tweak that can enhance the overall results.

- Personalization

Your web browser tracks the things you search for in the net. It knows your IP address and other saved data. It is also capable of storing your passwords if you allow it to store or keep your password (more about this subject on Chapter 15 about cyber criminals). Even if you are already searching for other subject matter but it has relevance to your previous search, it will yield search results that have something to do with your earlier quest.

You can avoid this issue when you delete your cookies. You can also choose to open an incognito window (where it has no record or history of your activities) and do your search.

- Area or Region

After the Google Pigeon update, people have noticed that they get different search results depending on their location. Your brand's reputation may look awful or bad in Boston and great in Chicago.

If you want to find out your search results in different areas, you can click 'Search Tools' and then replace your area with your preferred search location.

6. After six months there's still no result, is this normal?

It would take time before you can beat a negative result. Understand that you can only push it off the front page of the search results and make it practically invisible. However, if you can't see any improvement after six months, you may need to re-evaluate the situation. If you cannot find your web properties on the first three pages of the search results, it is time to try a different strategy. Perhaps, your chosen keyword is too competitive. You may need to re-evaluate the way your sites link to each other.

If you think that you have done everything you can and still can't see any change in your situation, you can seek some help from a SEO specialist.

7. What about publishing on third party publications?

Publishing your articles or content on third party publications can also help you with your online reputation management. There won't be a lot of articles about you or your company and you need to give people the right information. When you rely on journalists to write something about you, it is possible that they might divulge something irrelevant that could forever affect your reputation.

You are the best source of information regarding your business (or you can also try being the source for HARO as mentioned in Quick Steps in ORM for the Unsophisticated Net User). Getting your materials published on third party publications can also help supplement your campaign. Sometimes, the articles that you have written can give you an advantageous ranking. It is mostly due to its affiliation with you as its author.

8. Is it advisable to create more than one account in Twitter and LinkedIn?

Instead of creating double or triple accounts in Twitter, LinkedIn, and other social media, it is best to spend your spare time writing high quality content for your particular profile. Maintaining too many accounts under one social media is a waste of time. You need to give the same amount of work to maintain the accounts. You also need to make sure to update them regularly. It is enough that you have one account per social media (choose the most popular ones (suggestions were given in the past chapter).

9. If the negative result is pushed out of the first page, is it considered a success?

You can consider it a success because less than 10% of net surfers go to the succeeding pages of search results. Most people think that only the first page of the search results can offer the information they need. However, you must continue to rank your properties to push out the negative search results further until they become practically non-existent.

You also need to keep in mind that some of the negative materials about you or your brand can bounce back. You must remain consistent in providing fresh content to your customers and followers. It is also important to update your social media on regular basis and let your followers to always feel your online presence and you are always there for them.

10. Is it okay to be complacent if there's no negative search result?

You should not be complacent just because you don't have any negative search result. You need to continue managing your online reputation and make sure that it remains good all the time. You will never when someone tries to do unscrupulous means to ruin your online reputation. Don't let that person have the opportunity to slander you. Make your good online reputation rigid by making sure that your web properties gain more authority. It would be difficult for someone who wants to slander your good name to carry out his/her plans.

In the 2014 statistics, about 80% of employers rely on Google to know more about a certain job applicant before inviting him/her for an interview. That's why it is recommended to constantly monitor your online reputation. If you have a sturdy reputation, those people who want to bring you down can do everything they can to do so but will still fail in the end.

While you don't have negative search results (yet), do everything to keep your online reputation in great shape all the time.

The information in this chapter plus the other things that you've learned in the previous chapters can help you a lot in managing your online reputation. It is also great to have good time management, so you can prioritize the things that need your immediate attention. You also need to properly delegate the work and choose the most capable person for a particular task.

Chapter 14: The dark side of Online Reputation Management

Running a Online Reputation Management company always meant for us to do the right thing, keep our ethical values and refuse any work that was against our values. Although we know tools that could be used for faster results, we have never offered them to any of our clients and we advocate against the existence of such tools.

The goal of this book was to help you boost your online reputation and we also wanted to share some secrets so we can fight against those techniques and be alert for their existence. On the previous chapters we shared legal practices but on this chapter, you will show what some unscrupulous ORM companies do.

Remember, we do not encourage any person to use those tools and we advocate against their use. The more people know about the risks of these tools, the more laws we can have against it to protect us.

The Persuasion Network

The persuasion network is a technique that envolves a number of fake users with names, personalities, sites and social media accounts. These accounts pretend to be avid advocate for a brand or person and they create blogs with a large positive content, they are the first to share and like social media posts and they are the first to fight back when a negative review or comment pops up. Those account can be used to support attacks from one of the accounts and they are even used to threat people that leave negative comments.

Sometimes, persuasion networks even works creating fake news media sites that look extremely reputable and they use these sites to create and spread fake news.

The persuasion network is a unethical practice that can also be used to bully competitors. Hackers take advantage of their anonymity on the internet to create many fake social profiles and harass people.

Kali Linux

Kali Linux is a operational system based on the Linux distribution that comes with many software tools for cyber security testing.

When you have visited forums that discuss things about Kali Linux tools, you may think that the said tools can be considered the best buddies of ethical and scrupulous hackers. There are people who think that once they learned how to use the Kali Linux tools, they can go on a hacking spree. To be honest, it is not like that at all. Hackers that bring trouble to others and gain monetary benefits by making the victims miserable are also called cyber criminals. Yes, such act of hacking is a crime.

TV shows that elevate the hackers' status to a new height due to their ability to crack certain codes could be responsible for the wrong image that people have about them. Young minds are usually influenced into thinking that hacking is cool and most of them would like to be a hacker when they grow up. Understand that hacking requires skills, knowledge, and right attitude to pull it off.

You need to understand that hacking should be the last resort if everything else fails. Since there are bad hackers, the term ethical hacker was born. The term aims to differentiate the experts who are doing things legally from the cyber criminals who can hack the systems.

Kali Linux's Tools

Kali is actually a set of bundled testing tools for web systems. Each tool comes with its own sub-tools and options. To all the Kali Linux tools efficiently, you need to know the uses of each tool and how to operate it. If you are unfamiliar with Linux, it is best to learn it first before you tinker with the Kali Linux tools.

The tools are useful to forensic experts, pentesters, and hackers. The said people who already discovered the ingenious uses of the Kali tools always keep them handy.

The Kali Linux tools are already bundled up and ready to run. You don't need to download anything to make the tools work. You don't even need to install and configure the tools before you use them. You can use them at any given time.

It is constantly updated and has an amazing support community. It appears to do better in live mode than offline. It is also fast.

However, there are certain disadvantages of Kali and one of them is that it might not always work or would only work for particular configurations. It does not fit to be a day to day desktop operating system. It is not advisable to play video games on Kali.

We'll go over briefly some tools we know Kali has and the possibilities it opens for cyber criminals looking into erasing the content of website they don't own, creating fake news and even invading servers and websites.

Information Gathering

There are softwares for information gathering like Maltego that can search for emails, contacts, phone numbers and many other information from a company or person in order to gather information to create a personalized attack, email contact or to try to pretend to be someone known.

Exploitation Tools

Kali offers softwares that scan servers and sites searching for known vulnerabilities. If they find any, some software even offer the option to attack the server or the web application running on the server. Those kind of tools are used by unscrupulous hackers to gain access over a server and change data or even bring the whole server down. One of examples of application like this is Armitage.

Password Cracking

Kali also has software to try to crack passwords using some techniques like dictionary attacks - which tries to combine a word list usually gathered from Information Gathering software to make as much personalized as possible.

Social Engineering Tools

After gathering information from a specific target using Information Gathering tools on Kali Linux and also on social media, a malicious hacker can spoof an email pretending to be someone the target know and asking to change information on a website or even asking to download a file or click on a link.

There are cases that hackers even go to a cafe next to a newspaper where he can harvest information and login from employees by installing cameras or fake wifi spots.

Downloading a malicious file or clicking on a malicious link can authorize hackers to connect to your computers giving them full access to your data, to store keyboard inputs and even to see your screen and your camera.

Spoofing email can also contain links to a fake website. SET is a application from Kali that even allows hackers to copy sites like banks, social media logins pages and many more sites in less than a minute and offer a server with a link that can be sent a target. The target will then navigate to a fake address and pass his credentials to a target thinking that he is logging in to his account.

Below, you will find the different Kali Linux tools and they are grouped according to their uses. You will notice that some of the tools are under one or more uses. If you want to be proficient in using the different tools, take time to learn them and make sure to train yourself in using them.

List of Kali Linux Tools and their Uses

Here is a list of Kali Linux tools and where you can use them:

INFORMATION GATHERING TOOLS			
Xplico	SMBMap	InSpy	dnswalk
WOL-E	SET	ident-user-enum	dnstracer
Wireshark	Recon-ng	hping3	DNSRecon
URLCrazy	Parsero	goofile	dnsmap
twofi	p0f	GoLismero	dnsenum
TLSSLed	OSRFramework	Ghost Phisher	dnmap
theHarvester	ntop	fragrouter	DMitry

THC-IPV6	Nmap	fragroute	copy-router-config
Sublist3r	nbtscan-unixwiz	Firewalk	Cookie Cadger
SSLyze	Miranda	Fierce	cisco-torch
sslstrip	Metagoofil	Faraday	CDPSnarf
SSLsplit	masscan	EyeWitness	CaseFile
sslcaudit	Maltego Teeth	enumIAX	braa
SPARTA	lbd	enum4linux	bing-ip2hosts
snmp-check	iSMTP	DotDotPwn	Automater
smtp-user-enum	InTrace	Amap	arp-scan
ace-voip	acccheck		

EXPLOITATION TOOLS

Yersinia	MSFPC	crackle	BeEF
THC-IPV6	Metasploit Framework	Commix	Backdoor Factory
sqlmap	Maltego Teeth	cisco-torch	Armitage
ShellNoob	Linux Exploit Suggester	cisco-ocs	cisco-auditing-tool
SET	jboss-autopwn	cisco-global-exploiter	exploitdb
Router Sploit			

TOOLS FOR WIRELESS ATTACKS

wpaclean	RTLSDR Scanner	hostapd-wpe	mfterm

Wifite	redfang	gr-scan	mfoc
Wifitap	Reaver	Gqrx	mfcuk
wifiphisher	Pyrit	GISKismet	mdk3
Wifi Honey	PixieWPS	Ghost Phisher	makeivs-ng
Wesside-ng	Packetforge-ng	FreeRADIUS-WPE	Kismet
Tkiptun-ng	Multimon-NG	Fern Wifi Cracker	KillerBee
Spooftooph	Bully	Easside-ng	kalibrate-rtl
Airmon-ng	Bluesnarfer	eapmd5pass	ivstools
coWPAtty	BlueRanger	crackle	Airolib-ng
Aireplay-ng	Bluepot	BlueMaho	Airodump-ng
Airdecap-ng and Airdecloak-ng	airodump-ng-oui-update	Airtun-ng	Bluelog

Aircrack-ng	Asleap	Airserv-ng	Besside-ng
Airbase-ng			

TOOLS FOR WEB APPLICATIONS

WebSlayer	Parsero	Skipfish	
Webshag	Paros	Recon-ng	PadBuster
WebScarab	FunkLoad	ProxyStrike	Maltego Teeth
zaproxy	plecost	Powerfuzzer	jSQL Injection
XSSer	w3af	fimap	joomscan
WPScan	Vega	DirBuster	jboss-autopwn
Wfuzz	Uniscan	DIRB	hURL
WebSploit	ua-tester	deblaze	Grabber
Burp Suite	sqlsus	DAVTest	Gobuster

BlindElephant	Sqlninja	CutyCapt	Arachni
BBQSQL	sqlmap	apache-users	

STRESS TESTING TOOLS

inviteflood	DHCPig	Reaver	Termineter
ipv6-toolkit	FunkLoad	rtpflood	THC-IPV6
mdk3	iaxflood	SlowHTTPTest	THC-SSL-DOS
Inundator	t50		

REPORTING TOOLS

Dradis	Metagoofil	RDPY	cherrytree
dos2unix	MagicTree	pipal	CaseFile
CutyCapt	Nipper-ng		

SNIFFING AND SPOOFING TOOLS

rtpmixsound	Burp Suite	sslstrip	iSMTP
rtpinsertsound	zaproxy	SSLsplit	inviteflood
rtpbreak	Yersinia	SniffJoke	iaxflood
responder	xspy	SIPVicious	HexInject
rebind	Wireshark	SIPp	hamster-sidejack
protos-sip	Wifi Honey	SIPArmyKnife	fiked
ohrwurm	WebScarab	sctpscan	DNSChef
mitmproxy	VoIPHopper	THC-IPV6	isr-evilgrade

TOOLS FOR PASSWORD ATTACKS

SQLdict	Johnny	crowbar	PACK
RSMangler	John the Ripper	creddump	ophcrack
rcracki-mt	HexorBase	zaproxy	oclgaussrack
RainbowCrack	hash-identifier	wordlists	Ncrack
polenum	Hashcat	WebScarab	multiforcer
phrasendrescher	gpp-decrypt	TrueCrack	Maskprocessor
patator	findmyhash	THC-pptp-bruter	Maltego Teeth
CmosPwd	DBPwAudit	THC-Hydra	keimpx
cisco-auditing-tool	crunch	Statsprocessor	BruteSpray

chntpw	CeWL	Burp Suite	acccheck

TOOLS FOR MAINTAINING ACCESS

RidEnum	Winexe	Intersect	CryptCat
pwnat	Weevely	http-tunnel	Cymothoa
PowerSploit	Webshells	HTTPTunnel	sbd
polenum	U3-Pwn	dns2tcp	dbd
Nishang	shellter		

REVERSE ENGINEERING TOOLS

YARA	jad	dex2jar	OllyDbg
Valgrind	edb-debugger	apktool	JD-GUI

| smali | diStorm3 | javasnoop | |

HARDWARE HACKING TOOLS

smali	dex2jar	apktool
Sakis3G	Arduino	android-sdk

You may need to check online every now and then for updates on Kali Linux tools. They may have new additional tools that you can use.

Chapter 15: Cyber Criminals and Your Online Reputation

There are times when different cyber threats can bring havoc to your internet or online presence, especially when someone paid the cyber criminals to toy with your computer or web properties. Right this moment, are you sure you are internet safe?

Know that there are different ways or methods that hackers employ to get your information and have the power to alter your image or online presence. You must have heard about some cases where Facebook accounts had been hacked and the hacker create anger-inducing posts that can ruin the reputation of the account owner. There are many cases of hacking that bring trouble to the account owner. Big and small businesses employ the services of cyber security experts to make sure that the security of their network is intact.

Do you keep records of your customers' personal information in your computer or network? How do you keep them safe? How do you keep your personal information safe? These are just some of the questions that you need to consider for your cyber security. You are partly responsible for keeping the personal information of your customers safe and secure. Although, there are cases where the customers themselves are the ones who failed to protect their own personal information.

Your online reputation can be ruined under the scheming ways of a hacker. But, an efficient and reliable cyber security can shield you from the cyber criminal's attempt to breach your security and do some damage to you and your business as well as your customers.

If you have a flourishing business, it is advisable to have a security team that can protect the integrity of your computer network. Having a reliable security is good, having an efficient software and dependable security team is way even better. You need to constantly update your security software to make sure that it will be able to take on the new breed of malware and viruses that may suddenly attack your computer system.

Aside from having a reliable cyber security, there are also things that you can do to protect yourself online. You can also tell your customers to do the same.

Tip #1: Don't Simply Click

Are you someone who always click first and ponder later? Most people are like that and it is something that can bring you trouble. Cyber criminals use every means that can help them get through the account or computer system of their target.

If you received an unknown email and looks a bit odd, don't open it. Take a closer look at its origin and the complete email address. If the sender is unfamiliar, don't open it. If you do and you see that it contains a link, don't click on the link.

Cyber criminals include links in their email that would redirect the recipient to a certain website or activate a malware. When that happens, the cyber criminal can manipulate or take over the recipient's account and do other unscrupulous things, including ruining the owner's reputation.

Plus emails can be spoofed to seem like a relative, a colleague or a friend is sending you an email.

To give you an idea on how web-based attacks happen, here is a list of steps that typically occur:

1. A cyber criminal may choose a decent, legit website to introduce a malicious link.

2. The regular visitors of that website will surely drop by to see the latest things that the website has to offer.

3. The malicious URL that cyber criminal has planted on the website will redirect the visitors to a bad website that can determine the operating system of the people who got redirected. It can also detect the browser that the visitor uses and the plugins that are vulnerable.

4. The unscrupulous website will automatically download and install a malicious code to the computer of his victim. Once the downloaded content is activated, the hacker gets his chance to take over the victim's computer.

5. The malware will attack the vulnerable media player right away. A cyber criminal may install a dozen or more malware files to the computer of the victim.

6. The malware attacks the victim's computer system and gather personal data, which it sends to the hacker. The important data could be bank account information, passwords, and others.

If the cyber criminal wants to ruin your reputation, he could introduce the malicious link to your website, so he can take control of the personal information of your customers that visit your website. He will surely do something dishonest with the accounts. One way or the other, your customers will know that their recent trouble was due to the malware in your website. Whether or not you're the one who put it there, in the minds of your customers you are responsible, and you just got them in trouble.

Tip #2: Be Wary of Your Employees or Business Partners

There are also insider threats that you should worry about. As the name implies, an insider threat is committed by someone who can personally access the company's important data or file. He can send those data to the hacker or do something about it himself.

If your employee or business partner is trying to access a restricted area or company file, it is possible that he is planning to do something to your business. You can tell your

IT security team to restrict employees and business partners from accessing sensitive data. You can also ask your IT team to design or install a software that can monitor the online or computer activities of your employees.

You can also choose to put CCTV for added security.

Tip #3: Train Your Employees

There are times when employees inadvertently cause the breach in your computer system. You need to train them to be careful of the different means that cyber criminals may use to penetrate your computer network. They usually employ phishing tactics, which can be easily accomplished when the recipient of a malicious email clicks the link it contains.

Sometimes, an employee's negligence can put the entire business in trouble. Make your employees understand the meaning behind teamwork and let them feel that each of one is an important part of the company. They should always be careful in everything they do or say.

Tip #4: Safeguard Login Credentials

Tell your customers to safeguard their login credentials whenever they use a computer in a net café. Cyber criminals are everywhere. No one can tell whether the gentleman that sits next to your customer in a net café is a cyber criminal or not. He could be waiting for his chance to steal the password of your customer and do something illegal with the account.

Also make sure logins, passwords and credit card information are properly stored and preserved.

For any critical login, use 2-step authentication process. You can search on how to enable it for each platform that holds sensitive information.

Severity of Cyber Crimes

You should not take cyber crimes lightly and it is foolish to think that they won't be interested in attacking you. Well, there's a hint of truth in that but your competitors or one of them might hire a hacker to do the dirty work. It is also possible that you may lose more than your good reputation. You may lose your entire business.

If the statements above did not convince you, take a look at the following facts:

- 60% of small companies completely ceased its operation after suffering a huge blow from a cyber attack.

- Only 14% of small businesses can honestly say that they have effective and efficient ways to counter cyber attacks and minimize system risks and weaknesses.

- 43% of cyber assaults are directed at small companies.

- 48% of data security infraction was caused by malicious intent, and the rest can be blamed on human error and/or system malfunction.

- Companies that suffered from cyber attacks confirmed that: 49% were inflicted with web-based attack, 43% fought with social engineering or phishing attacks, 35% suffered from general malware, 26% experienced SQL injection, 21% encountered denial-of-service or DoS, 13% had malicious insider, and 11% had some trouble dealing with cross-site scripting.

The cyber attacks can jeopardize the entire business operation and cause delays and other issues that can lead to customers' dissatisfaction. Expect negative reviews and comments to pop up and they will surely affect your online reputation.

You can only apologize and explain everything properly and assure your customers that you're already on top of everything. Assure them that you and your team are doing everything you can to bring everything back to normal at the soonest time possible. You also need to assure your customers that you have a tighter security that can deal with anything that the cyber criminal tries to do. Just make sure that you really have the kind of cyber security that can handle the attacks.

Don't let your guard down even for a second after you've been attacked. It is possible that the cyber criminal would attack once more while you are still weak. It is also possible that another cyber offender might suddenly attack you right after being attacked.

How to Detect Possible Cyber Attack

You can detect when your computer system is under attack, but you need to be observant to detect it. Here are some of the signs that you need to watch out for:

- Unexpected messages or images that pop on your computer screen.

- Your computer's security system warns that an application is trying to set up a net connection.

- Your friends, family, customers, or acquaintances inform or ask you about a certain email that you never sent.

- Your computer begins to freeze suddenly and frequently or each application that you try to run seems to go slower than before.

- You receive a lot of system error messages.

- Your operating system does not load right away or not at all when you turn on your computer.

- There are files and folders that are missing or modified.

- The web browser is having an abnormal, weird behavior.

To avoid cyber attacks, it is important to have a dependable cyber security all the time. Make it a habit to monitor the activities of your computer system and if you detect something is wrong, report it immediately to the IT security team of the company.

Chapter 16: Report Content

As you will see below, not all entities comprising the World Wide Web currently has systems, tools, and countermeasures in place to address the spread of fake news, cyberbullying, illegal and inappropriate content. However, some of them are now working to put measures in place. Let's starts with the big names in social media.

FACEBOOK

At the time of this writing, users can report a abusive content by following these steps:

On the post, click the … in the upper right corner.

Select the 'Give feedback on this video' option.

Select the 'False News' option.

Click the 'Send' button.

TWITTER

Twitter users are left with the classic option of reporting something abusive or harmful. Here's what you can do:

Click the chevron icon

Choose the 'Report Tweet' option

Choose spam from the radio button options

Click 'Next'

Choose your preferred course of action

Click 'Done.'

You can choose to read more about Twitter's How to Report a Spam and How to Report Violations.

INSTAGRAM

To report a spam or abuse, people can do two things: they can report a specific post or they can report an entire profile.

To report a post:

Tap on the three dots above the post

Tap 'Report'

Follow the onscreen instructions

To report a profile:

Tap on the three dots above the profile page

Tap 'Report'

Follow the onscreen instructions

For more information, people can refer to Instagram's Abuse & Spam page.

LINKEDIN

Yes, a social media network devoted to professionals can also be a target for the abusive content. And LinkedIn has a comprehensive set of instructions for people to follow when it comes to reporting Inappropriate Messages, Inappropriate Content, or Safety Concerns. Let's take a look at each of them.

Fake Profiles

Fake profiles can be pages that impersonate other people, empty profiles, profiles with fake names, or profiles that contain profanity. To report a fake profile:

Click the ... icon on the member's profile

Click the Report/Block icon

Select 'Report this profile' in the 'What do you want to do?' pop-up window.

Select the applicable reason for flagging the profile in the 'Tell us a little more' pop-up window.

Click 'Submit'

Inaccurate Profiles

Inaccurate profiles also fall within the realm of fake news. While 'inaccurate' is used, some people deliberately include details about their personal or professional background that are entirely fabricated. To report an inaccurate profile, a formal complaint must be launched by using LinkedIn's 'Notice of Inaccurate Profile Information' form.

Hacked Accounts

Hacked accounts can be used as mediums to spread disinformation. As a consequence, the real person behind the profile may end up being totally discredited. At times, one person may feel that one of his or her connection's account is hacked. For both, the process of reporting can be found in the Reporting a Hacked Account page.

Scams

Fake information used with the intention to scam people are also in place on LinkedIn. There are four types of scams the social media platform recognizes:

Inheritance or advance fee fraud scams, which is characterized by LinkedIn as, 'scams [that] usually request a small fee up front in order to receive a large sum of money in return.

Job scams characterized as involving 'people pretending to be recruiters or employers offering high-paying jobs for little work. These can include mystery shopper, work from home or personal assistant scams.'

Technical support scams as offers for help from within LinkedIn with a corresponding fee.

Dating and romance scams coming from people who contact other people expressing interest in a romantic relationship. For this one, it should be noted that LinkedIn was established as a professional platform and not as a dating site.

To report any of these types of scams, you can follow the instructions on the Recognizing and Reporting Scams page.

LinkedIn also has a dedicated reporting feature its acquisition, SlideShare which can be found on the Flagging Inappropriate Content on SlideShare.

YOUTUBE

Google's video-sharing platform application, YouTube, could be a little late in joining the fight-fake-news bandwagon. Nonetheless, it announced specific plans in early 2018 on how to combat the proliferation of fake content within its platform, among others. But right now, the process in place to report a video with fake content is as follows:

Click the ... on the lower right corner of a video.

Choose 'Report.'

Tick the applicable radio button.

Choose from the dropdown fields.

Click 'Next.'

Follow the onscreen prompts.

TUMBLR

In a news report published by The Guardian in March 2018, it revealed that Tumblr has uncovered 84 accounts linked to 13 people who are affiliated with a Russia's Internet Research Agency. The IRA is a troll farm and was known to have an influence over the US 2016 presidential elections.

In response, Tumblr said that it will be sending an emailing anyone who followed an IRA-linked account, who liked, who replied to, or who reblogged any posts linked to the IRA. However, it said that users will still have an option on whether or not to delete the content from their account. The email will only serve to inform.

Tumblr also mentioned that apart from the email, it will also be maintaining a record of all IRA-linked usernames on a publicly accessible database.

Finally, the report also quotes Tumblr saying that it [Tumblr] 'is committed to terminating accounts in the future if it finds them to be affiliated with "disinformation campaigns," and alerting law enforcement of their identities. "Be aware that people want to manipulate the conversation," the post reads. "Knowing that disinformation and propaganda accounts are out there makes it harder for them to operate.'

GOOGLE

Among all others mentioned in this chapter, perhaps Google is experiencing the most pressure when it comes to its efforts in combatting abusive content. Google is not just the search engine, but also Youtube, Google Shopping, Google Play Apps, Blogger and Blogspot.

Google has a page where you can ask to remove content called "Removing Content from Google" on this URL https://support.google.com/legal/troubleshooter/1114905?hl=en. There is also more information for Legal Requests on this

page:
https://support.google.com/legal/answer/3110420?hl=en.

Final Words

Thank you again for downloading this book!

If you want to ensure your company's success, you need to develop a good online reputation before you even begin operating your business. You need to design an efficient online reputation management that can help a lot in keeping negative comments, reviews, content, and other unfavorable materials from popping up or keep them under control.

Negative search result can bring trouble, but the lack of it may make the public doubt you even more. Everyone is aware that even the best company has negative publicity under their name. Since not all people have the same preferences, not all will like the same things. The things that you are satisfied with may not be the same as your friend's. You may share common interests, but not always. People know that every business has negative search result, and you should have your share too. But, you need to make sure that such negative content won't severely affect your reputation.

The book has given you a vast collection of helpful information and tips to manage your online reputation and keep negative content (including reviews and comments) at bay. Remember to always value your customers and make them feel special all the time by making them aware that you take their comments and reviews with an open mind. Make them understand that you value their opinions and views. Let them see that you and your team are doing your best to give them the best customer experience that they can ever have.

You may consider negative search result as a letdown but take comfort in the fact that failure is something that enhances the sweet taste of success. **So keep failing, fail fast and fail often, fail your way to success.**

Now that you understand the good and the bad on online reputation management, help us fight against unscrupulous and manipulative techniques on the internet to make sure we can create a better future for the generations to come.

If you enjoyed this book, please take the time to share your thoughts and post a review on Amazon. It'd be greatly appreciated!

Thank you and good luck!

Fernando Uilherme Barbosa de Azevedo

www.ingramcontent.com/pod-product-compliance
Lightning Source LLC
Chambersburg PA
CBHW031422210526
45464CB00005B/2015